Jim E

Cracking the Rich Code^6

Inspiring Stories, Insights and Strategies from Entrepreneurs Around the World

STAY IN TOUCH WITH JIM AND KEVIN

www.JimBritt.com

www.JimBrittCoaching.com

www.CrackingTheRichCode.com

www.KevinHarringtom.tv

For daily strategies and insights from top entrepreneurs, join us at

THE RICH CODE CLUB

FREE members site.

www.TheRichCodeClub.com

Co-authors from Around the World

Jim Britt

Kevin Harrington

Amy Bolding

Andrea Adams-Miller

Rich Kozak

Tara L Killen

Judy Copenbarger

Arline Warwick

Edith Gondwe

Dawna Campbell

Shenal Arimilli

Frida Bruhn

Andria Barrett

David Chametzky

Careyann Zivich

Janelle Cameron

Pamela Chanel David

Rhonda Grant

Yolanda Martinez

Julie Rivera

Bryan Standish

Greg Herlean

DEDICATION

Entrepreneurs will change the world. They always have and they always will.

To the entrepreneurial spirit that lives within each of us.

God Bless America and the World!

Foreword by Kevin Harrington

You probably know me as one of the "Sharks" on the hit TV show Shark Tank, where I was an investor in many entrepreneurial ventures. But my life and business weren't always like that. I used to be your regular, everyday guy patching cracked driveways to make money. I had hopes and dreams just like most, yet I worked around people who didn't support my dreams. But you know what? I not only found a way out, but I found a way to my dreams... and so can you.

Now, I wake up every morning excited about my day, and I surround with only the people I want in my life; entrepreneurs who really want something more than just getting by paycheck to paycheck. Today we hear stories -- mostly from the mainstream media -- everyday about how bad things are, businesses are closing, and jobs being lost, interest rates are on the rise, how the gap between rich and poor is growing and how you'll never make it on your own. But here's what I know for sure. Entrepreneurs are going to change the world. We always have and we always will. Forget the 1% vs the 99%. 100% of us entrepreneurs need answers. We need solutions. We need something more than what we're being told by those who don't have a clue. We need to start saying Yes! to opportunity and No! to all the noise. The fact is that it's a new world and a new economy. The "proven" methods of doing business and investing that produced successful results, even two years ago, simply may not work anymore.

If you want to succeed (or even survive) in our new world, you need an entirely new set of skills and information.

You need to "reposition" yourself...often.

You need to revamp how you do business...often.

You need to change how you handle and invest your money...often.

Like any other situation, if you know WHAT to do and WHEN to do it, you'll not only be "safe"... you could easily skyrocket financially.

If you have the right knowledge for today, the right opportunities for today, the right strategies for today and most of all the right character and mindset for today, you can win — and you can win big!

What I've discovered in my over three-decade career as an entrepreneur, is that success in the face of financial adversity boils down to 3 things:

The right knowledge at the right time.

The right opportunities at the right time.

The right you... ALL the time.

The bottom line is this: you can no longer afford to rely on anyone else to navigate your financial future. You have to rely on your "self." The question is... do you have a "self" you can rely on? Unfortunately, when it comes to entrepreneurship and money, many people don't. They don't have the financial education, the mental toughness, the knowledge and the skills to build wealth... especially in an ever-changing marketplace. You need to get RE-educated. You need to REINVENT yourself for success in the new economy. You need to learn new strategies in the areas of business and career, finance and real estate that create wealth or at least financial freedom in today's new world. But that's not all...

Skills and strategies and all that profound new knowledge won't do you one bit of good if you don't have the CHARACTER, the HABITS and the MENTALITY it takes to get rich. If you have internal barriers, your road to success will be slow and full of pain and struggle. It's like driving with one foot on the gas and one foot on the brake and always wondering why you aren't getting anywhere. Your mind is working against you instead of for you.

I have seen business owners come to me with their business ready to go under — and have the next year be their best financial year ever. I've seen others that had a business that should skyrocket yet fail because they didn't have the mental toughness to go the distance. I have seen people stuck in dead-end, dreary jobs break out of their rut, get involved in a brand-new passion, and become wildly successful.

No matter what you do for a living...regardless of your education, level of business experience or current financial status...If you have a burning desire for financial change then you won't want to miss this rare opportunity to learn from the entrepreneurs within this book.

It will provide you with some of the same success strategies that Jim Britt and I have used personally and shared with tens of thousands of people who've had tremendous financial success...people just like you, who wanted to get out of the rat race and enjoy financial freedom.

In addition, you'll learn what others have done, mistakes they made and how you can avoid them. You'll discover strategies that could make your business into a major market leader. I always say, "Just one good idea can change everything."

Success is predictable if you know what determines it. This book offers some valuable tips, knowledge, insights, skill sets, that will challenge you to leap beyond your current comfort level. If you want to strengthen your life, your business and your effectiveness overall, you'll discover a great friend in this book. You'll probably want to recommend it to all your entrepreneurial friends.

Although I haven't followed Jim Britt's career over the last 40 years, but I do know that he is recognized as one of the top thought leaders in the world, helping millions of people create prosperous lives. He has authored 13 books and multiple programs showing people how to understand their hidden abilities to do more, become more and enjoy more in every area of life. I also want to recognize Joel Sauceda, our online business partner. He is the brains behind the many online PR, Marketing, Branding and Lead Generation strategies each entrepreneur coauthor and reader of the book will benefit from.

The principles, concepts and ideas within this book are sometimes simple, but can be profound to a person who is ready for that perfect message at the right time and is willing to take action to change. Maybe for one it's a chapter on leadership or mindset. For the next, it's a chapter on raising capital, or securing a business loan. Each chapter is like opening a surprise empowering gift.

The conclusion to me is an exciting one. You, me and every other human being are shaping our brains and bodies by our attitude, the decisions we make, the intentions we hold and the actions we take daily. Why is it exciting? Because we are in control of all these things and we can change as long as we have the intention, willingness and commitment to look inside, take charge of our lives and make the changes.

I want to congratulate Jim Britt for making this publication series available and for allowing me to write the foreword, a chapter in each book and be involved with the entrepreneurs within this book and series. I honor Jim and the coauthors within this book and the series for the lives they are changing.

As you enter these pages, do so slowly and with an open mind. Savor the wisdom you discover here, and then with interest and curiosity discover what rings true for you, and then take action toward the life you want.

So many people settle for less in life, but I can tell you from my experience that it doesn't have to be that way.

Be prepared…because your life and business, is about to change!

Jim Britt & Kevin Harrington

As co-creators of this book series Jim Britt and Kevin Harrington have devoted their lives to helping others to live a more prosperous, fulfilled and happy life. Over the years they have influenced millions of lives through their coaching, mentoring, business strategies and leading by example. They are committed to never ending self-improvement and an inspiration to all they touch. They are both a true example that all things are possible. If you get a chance to work with Kevin and Jim or becoming a coauthor in a future Cracking the Rich Code book, jump at the chance!

Table of Contents

Jim Britt

Jim Britt is an award-winning author of 15 best-selling books and six #1 International best-sellers. Some of his many titles include Rings of Truth, Do This. Get Rich-For Entrepreneurs, Unleashing Your Authentic Power, The Power of Letting Go, Cracking the Rich Code and The Entrepreneur.

He is an internationally recognized business and life strategist who is highly sought after as a keynote speaker, both online and live, for all audiences.

As an entrepreneur Jim has launched 28 successful business ventures. He has served as a success strategist to over 300 corporations worldwide and was recently named as one of the world's top 50 speakers and top 20 success coaches. He was presented with the "Best of the Best" award out of the top 100 contributors of all time to the Direct Selling industry.

In the past 44 years Jim has presented seminars throughout the world sharing his success strategies and life enhancing realizations with over 5,000 audiences, totaling almost 2,000,000 people from all walks of life.

Early in his speaking career he was Business partners with the late Jim Rohn for eight years, where Tony Robbins worked under Jim's direction for his first few years in the speaking business.

As a performance strategist, Jim leverages his skills and experience as one of the leading experts in peak performance, entrepreneurship and personal empowerment to produce stellar results. He is pleased to work with small business entrepreneurs, and anyone seeking to remove the blocks that stop their success in any area of their life.

One of Jim's latest programs "Cracking the Rich Code" focuses on the subconscious programs influencing one's financial success www.CrackingTheRichCode.com

Think Like Superman

By Jim Britt

"Waking up to your true greatness in life requires letting go of who you imagine yourself to be." --- Jim Britt

FACT: Becoming a millionaire is easier than it has ever been.

Many people have the notion that it's an impossible task to become a millionaire. Some say, "It's pure luck." Others say, "You have to be born into a rich family." For others, "You'll have to win the Lotto." And for many they say, "Your parents have to help you out a lot." That's the language of the poor.

A single mother with five children says, "I want to believe in what you're saying. However, I'm 45 years old and work long hours at two dead-end jobs. I barely earn enough to get by. What should I do?"

Another man said, "Well, if you work for the government, you cannot expect to become a millionaire. After all, you're on a fixed salary and there's little time for anything else. By the time you get home, you've got to play with the kids, eat dinner, and fall asleep watching TV."

Everyone has a story as to why they could never become a millionaire. But for every story, excuse really, there are other stories OR PEOPLE with worse circumstances, that have become rich.

The truth is that all of us can become as wealthy as we decide to be, and that's a mindset. None of us is excluded from wealth. If you have the desire to receive money, whatever the amount, you have all of the rights to do so like everyone else. There is no limit to how much you can earn for yourself. The only limitations are what you place on yourself.

Money is like the sun. It does not discriminate. It doesn't say, "I will not give light and warmth to this flower, tree, or person because I don't like them." Like the sun, money is abundantly available to all of us who truly believe that it is for us. No one is excluded.

There are, however, some major differences between rich and poor people. Here are some tips for becoming rich.

Change Your Thinking

You have to see the bigger picture. There are opportunities everywhere! The problem is that most people see just trees, when they should be looking at the entire forest. By doing so you will see that there are opportunities everywhere. The possibilities are endless.

You'll also have to go through plenty of <u>self-discovery</u> before you earn your first million. Knowing the truth about yourself isn't always the easiest task. Sometimes, you'll find that you are your biggest enemy—at least some days.

Learn from Millionaires

Most people are surrounded by what I like to call their, "default friends." These friends are acquaintances that we see at the gym, school, work, local happy hour, and other places. We naturally befriend these people because we are all in the same boat financially. However, in most cases, these people aren't millionaires and cannot help you become one either. In fact, if you tell them you are going to become a millionaire, some may even tell you that it's impossible and discourage you from even trying. They'll tell you that you're living in a fantasy world and why you'll never be able to make it happen. Instead, learn from millionaires. Let go of these relationships that pull you down when it comes to your money desires. It's okay to have friends that aren't millionaires. However, only take input from those that have accomplished what you want to accomplish. Hang out with those that will encourage and help you get to the next level. Don't give your raw diamonds to a brick layer to be cut.

Indulge in Wealth

To become wealthy, you must learn about wealth. This means that you'll have to put yourself in situations that you've never been in before.

ON OCCASION, DO SOME OF THESE:

Fly first class and see how it makes you feel.

Eat out at the finest restaurant and don't look at the price.

Take a limo instead of a cab or Uber. Watch how you feel.

Reserve a suite in a first-class hotel.

If you are used to drinking a $20 bottle of wine, go for the $100 and see how it tastes. It does taste different.

All I am saying is, try some of the things that wealthy people do and see how it makes you feel.

Believe it is Possible

If you believe that it is possible to become a millionaire, you can make it happen. However, if you've excluded yourself from this possibility and think and believe that it's for other people, you'll never become a millionaire.

Also, be sure to bless rich people when you can. Haters of money aren't likely to receive any of it either.

Read books that have been written by millionaires. By gaining a well-rounded education about earning large sums of money and staying inspired, you'll be able to learn the wealth secrets of the rich. I just saw a video on LinkedIn with my friend Kevin Harrington from the TV show Shark Tank. He said that one of his new companies just had a million-dollar day on Amazon.

Enlarge Your Service

Your material wealth is the sum of your total contribution to society. Your daily mantra should be, *'How do I deliver more value to more people in less time?'* Then, you'll know that you can always increase your quality and quantity of service. Enlarging your service is also about going the extra mile. When it comes to helping others, you must give it everything you have. You just plant the seeds and nature will take care of the rest.

Seize ALL Opportunities That Make Sense

You cannot say "No" to opportunities and expect to become a millionaire. You must seize every opportunity that has your name on it. It may just be an opportunity to connect with an influential person for no reason. Sometimes the monetary reward will not come immediately, but if you keep planting seeds, eventually you'll grow a fruitful crop. Money is the harvest of the service you provide and sometimes the connections you have. The more seeds you plant, the greater the harvest.

Have an Unstoppable Mindset

Want to know some of what my first mentor shared with me that took me from a broke factory worker, high school dropout, to millionaire?

First, he said, you have to start thinking like a wealthy, unstoppable person. You have to have a wealth mindset. He said that wealthy people think differently. He said, "I want you to start thinking like Superman!" Sounds crazy, right? Well, it's not. It's powerful and here's why. How you think will change your life.

Wealthy people think differently. They really do. And anyone can learn to think like the wealthy.

I'm not talking about positive thinking, Law of Attraction, or motivation. Let's get real. None of that stuff works anyway. Otherwise, we would all be rich and happy already. I'm talking about thinking based in quantum physics science. Once you understand and apply it, it will change your life. You will become unstoppable!

If there was any person, fictional or real, whose qualities you could instantly possess, who would that person be? Think about it. Personally, I would say that Superman is the perfect person. Now, you are probably thinking I have lost it right? Just stick with me here. I think you will like what you are about to hear.

Superman is a fictional superhero widely considered to be one of the most famous and popular action hero and an American cultural icon. I remember watching Superman every Saturday morning when I was a kid. I couldn't get enough. He was my hero!

Let's look at Superman's traits:

Superman is indestructible.

He is a man of steel.

He can stop a locomotive in its tracks.

Bullets bounce off him.

He is faster than a speeding bullet.

No one can bring him down.

He can leap tall buildings in a single bound. Great powers to have in this day-and-age, wouldn't you say? What else would you need?

Now, for all you females, don't worry, we have not left you out. There is also a female version of Superman, named Superwoman. She has the same powers as Superman.

Now, this is where it gets interesting. Let's first look at the qualities that Superman possesses that you want to make your own. And to make it simple, I will refer to Superman for the rest of this message, and you can replace with Superwoman if you are female.

Again:

Superman is powerful and fearless.

Superman is virtually indestructible—except for kryptonite of course.

Superman can stop bullets.

Superman has supernatural powers. He can see through walls.

Superman can stop a speeding locomotive.

Superman can stop a bullet.

Superman jumps into immediate action when troubles arise.

Superman can crash through barriers.

Superman can even change clothes in a phone booth in seconds. Not too many of those around anymore. You'll have to duck behind a building to change.

So, you're thinking right now, *'Ok, I know that Superman has incredible supernatural powers, how can that help me? What good will it do me to think I am Superman, a fictional character?'*

Here is where science comes in. This is the part where you will be amazed when you learn about the supernatural powers that you already possess! NO, REALLY!

Your brain makes certain chemicals called neuro peptides. These are literally the molecules of emotion, like love, fear, joy, passion, and so on. These molecules of emotion are not only contained in your brain they actually circulate throughout your cellular structure. They send out a signal, a frequency much like a radio station sending out a signal. For example, you tune to 92.5 and you get jazz. Tune to 99.6 and you get rock. And if you are just one decimal off, you get static. The difference is that your signal goes both ways. You are a sender and a receiver.

You put out a signal, a mindset, of confidence about your financial success and people, circumstances, and opportunities show up to support your success. When you put out a signal of doubt and uncertainty and you receive support for your doubt and uncertainty. You've been around someone that you didn't trust, or you felt less than positive just being in their presence, right? You have also been around people that inspire you. That's what I'm talking about. You are projecting a frequency, looking to resonate with the frequency you are transmitting.

Anyway, the amazing part about these cells of emotion is that they are intelligent. They are thinking cells. These cells are constantly eavesdropping on the conversation that you are having with yourself. That's right. They are listening to you! And others are listening to your cells as well. Others feel what you feel when they are around you.

Your unconscious mind, your cells, are listening in, waiting to adjust your behavior based on what they hear from you, their master. So just imagine what would happen if you started to think like Superman...or like a millionaire.

Here are some of the thoughts you might have during the day:

"The challenges I face day today are easily overcome, after all I am Superman."

"I am indestructible."

"I have incredible strength."

"Nothing can stop me.....NOTHING."

"I have supernatural powers and can overcome anything."

"I can accomplish anything I want when I put my mind to it."

"I can break through any barrier."

"I can and I will do whatever it takes to accomplish my goal."

"I fear nothing."

The trillions of thinking cells in your body and brain listen, and they create exactly what you tell them to create. Their mission is to complete the picture of the you they see and hear when you talk to them. They must obey. It's their job!

Since you are Superman, you cannot fail. Why? Your thinking cells are now sending out the right signal because you told them to. They are making you stronger, more successful, everyday! You have the ability to fight off all negativity, doubt, fear, and worry—nothing can stop you!

Superman has total confidence. So, your cells of emotion relating to confidence will now create more neuro peptide chemicals to promote feelings of power and confidence that others will feel in your presence.

Superman is fearless. So, your cells of emotion relating to fear will now create more neuro peptide chemicals to create feelings of courage. You are unstoppable!

And here's the key. Others will respond to you in the same way that you are talking to yourself.

If you are confident, others will have confidence in you.

You have thousands of thoughts every day. Make sure your thoughts are leading you in the direction you want to go. Make sure you are telling your cells a success story, and not a 'woe is me' story.

Most have been conditioned to think that creating wealth is difficult, or that it's only for the lucky few. What do you believe? It doesn't cost you any more to think like Superman; and it's much more inspiring!

Mediocrity cannot be an option if you decide to be wealthy and think like Superman.

Your decision, and communication with your cells, creates a mindset; that mindset influences how you show up.

None of that old type of thinking matters anymore…after all, you are Superman, and you can accomplish anything.

If you want wealth, you have to stretch yourself. You have to do the things that unsuccessful people are not willing to do. You have to say "yes" to opportunity, then figure out how to get the job done.

Maybe you are uncomfortable selling and asking for money. If that's the case, then learn sales and learn to ask for money every day until you feel comfortable asking for it. You will never have money if you don't learn to ask for it.

I've learned a lot in the past 40+ years as an entrepreneur. I've learned that in order to have more, you have to become more. I've also learned that if you are comfortable, you are not growing. I learned that I couldn't go from a nervous rookie speaker with minimal self-confidence to hosting TV shows and speaking in front of 5,000 people overnight. I simply wasn't ready. I grew into that, one speaking engagement at a time. Every time I finished a speaking engagement, I would ask myself, "How did I do, and how could I do it better?" I still do that today.

And I've learned from the hundreds of thousands of people I've trained, coached, and mentored that none of us can do something we don't believe is possible. It's not going to happen if you're not ready to step out of your comfort zone and stretch yourself.

This has led me to understand the single most important principle of wealth-building, that has meant the difference between poverty and riches for people since humans first traded for pelts.

Are you ready?

Come in just a little closer. Listen up!

Every income level requires a different you, a different mindset! If you think that $10,000 a month is a lot of money, then $100,000 a month will be completely out of reach. If you believe that having $5,000 in the bank would make you rich, then $50,000 won't miraculously appear. You will never earn more money than you believe is "a lot" of money.

What you do as a business is only a small part of becoming rich. In fact, there are thousands, if not tens of thousands, of ways to make money—and lots of it. What I've learned over the years is that, by focusing on who you want to become instead of what you need to do, you're going to multiply your chances of getting rich a hundredfold.

Ask anyone who's found a way to make a large sum of money legally, and he or she will tell you that it's not hard once you crack the code. And cracking the code starts with you and your mindset. The "code" to which I refer isn't a secret rite or ancient scroll. It's not even a secret. It's a certain way of thinking and believing in which you've trained your mind to see money-making ideas.

That's where you see a need in the marketplace, and you jump on the idea quickly. It might involve creating a new product; or, it may just be teaching others a special technique you've learned. It may even require raising capital to start a company or to market a product or idea on social media.

Don't Hold Back. You Have to Take Action to Change.

Start right now to imagine yourself as already having wealth. How would your life be? How would your day unfold? Start to own your wealth mindset now! The subconscious mind is unable to differentiate between actual fact and mere visualization. So, by imagining that you already have it, you're encouraging your subconscious mind to seek the ways and means to transform your imaginary feelings into the real thing.

Find yourself some mentors. Nobody has all the answers. Surround yourself with people that will support, inspire, and provide you with answers that keep you moving in the right direction. If you truly want to attain wealth, have a thriving business, or reach the top of your game in any endeavor, having a qualified mentor is essential.

Okay, lets come in for a landing …

It is absolutely essential to have a crystal-clear picture of what you want to accomplish before you begin. If you want to attain wealth, you must learn to operate without fear and with a sharply defined mental image of the outcome you want to attain. This comes from thinking like a wealthy person, (like Superman) making decisions like a wealthy person and being fearless (like Superman) when it comes to stepping out of your comfort zone. Look at the end result as something you're already prepared to do, you just haven't done it yet.

Think about this. Your success is something that you have been preventing; it's not something you have to struggle to make happen. The key is to not let fear, doubt, other people, or mind chatter push your success away. You'll find that the solutions taking you toward your goals will come to you in the most unexpected and sudden ways. You don't need the *perfect* plan first. What you need is a perfectly clear decision about your success, the right mindset, the right mentoring, and the ideal way to get you there will materialize.

The greatest transfer of wealth in the history of the human race is happening right now. Are you positioned to get your share?

Remember, in order to get a different result, you must do something different. In order to do something different you must know something different to do. And in order to know something different, you have to first suspect that your present methods need improving.

THEN, YOU HAVE TO BE WILLING TO DO SOMETHING ABOUT IT.

***

For more information on Jim's work:

www.JimBritt.com

http://JimBrittCoaching.com

www.facebook.com/jimbrittonline

www.linkedin.com/in/jim-britt

For free audio series www.RichCode1.com and www.RichCode2.com

To find out how to crack the rich code and change your subconscious programming regarding money: www.CrackingTheRichCode.com

Kevin Harrington

Kevin Harrington is an original shark from the hit TV show *Shark Tank* and a successful entrepreneur for more than forty years. He's the co-founding board member of the Entrepreneurs' Organization and co-founder of the Electronic Retailing Association. He also invented the infomercial. He helped make "But wait... There's more!" part of our cultural history. He's one of the pioneers behind the *As Seen on TV* brand, has heard more than 50,000 pitches, and launched more than 500 products generating more than $5 Billion in global sales. Twenty of his companies have generated more than $100 million in revenue each. He's also the founder of the *Secrets of Closing the Sale Master Class* inspired by the Master of sales—Zig Ziglar. He's the author of several bestselling books including *Act Now: How I Turn Ideas into Million Dollar Products, Key Person of Influence,* and *Put a Shark in Your Tank.*

Becoming A KPI

By Kevin Harrington

The Key Person of Influence (KPI) in any given industry is the leader. It is the leader of the business world, the leader of automobile dealerships, the leader of selling hats—you name it. In other words, being the KPI means being the go-to person. The crazy thing? Anyone can be a Key Person of Influence. Any entrepreneur can be a KPI, a doctor, a salesperson, anyone. Just follow five steps and you will be well on your way. What comes with being a Key Person of Influence is value, ideally a massive amount of money, and being the leader in your field. The KPI is the person who comes up in conversations when it relates to a certain product, business, company, industry, or field. This is the person others seek out, the go-to person. Being the Key Person of Influence is how I got on *Shark Tank*.

Here's the story: I got a phone call from Mark Burnett's company. Mark Burnett is a television producer. He produced shows like *Survivor* and *The Voice*. His office called to set up an appointment. Mark was starting up a new show and wanted me to go out to Los Angeles to talk business. I was curious as to how Mark Burnett's company found me, and why they reached out for my services. They told me it was because I was a Key Person of Influence. I was all over the internet as a result of everything I was doing. It was 2008, and I had been in the business for 25 years. I had created huge brands. I helped build Tony Little. I helped build Jack Lalanne. I helped build Food Saver. We did the NuWave Oven. We worked with people like George Foreman and countless others. The problem was, everybody knew the brands, which was good for business, but did nothing for my personal brand. Consumers knew about the Food Saver, they knew about Tony Little, and they knew about Jack Lalanne, but not everyone knew I was the guy behind all of these people. Nobody knew me.

At that point, I made a conscious effort to build my brand. I wanted to become the go-to person so I could get the hot products and the phone calls. I helped build Tony Little's business, but everyone called him; they weren't calling me. What's wrong with that picture?

Well, for one, I invested millions and millions of dollars of my own capital into Tony Little, and then he got all the phone calls. Shame on me for doing that, right? So, I decided to build my brand, and that's when I came out with my book, *Key Person of Influence*. I promoted myself by doing radio talk shows, TV shows, trade journals, speeches, etc. This is how I got on *Shark Tank*.

If I hadn't met Daniel Priestley, my book could have become *How To Become The Go-To Guy* because that's what I was looking to do, but Daniel very eloquently created this five-step system called the "Key Person of Influence." Realizing we were on to something, we co-authored and launched *Key Person of Influence*. Let's look now at the necessary steps to become a KPI.

Obtaining Customers

In 1984, I started a business of obtaining customers on TV. One evening, I was watching the Discovery Channel and suddenly the channel went dark for about six hours. I then called the cable company just in case there was a problem. They told me there wasn't a problem, that the Discovery Channel was an 18-hour network. That's when the light bulb went off. This was downtime. They put no value on those six down hours. Instead of showing something during this time, bars were put up on the screen. I started thinking about what I could put in place of that downtime, to sell something, obtain customers, and make money. I'm like the Rembrandt TV guy. I created and invented the whole concept of going to TV stations and buying huge blocks of remnant downtime. In all these years of me doing this, no one has challenged the idea that I was the person who did it, created it, and invented 30-minute infomercial blocks.

I was buying big blocks of time. Why? Because I wanted to obtain customers. How do you obtain customers? A lot of ways, but you ultimately have to get some form of media. How does it start? There are two metrics you have to look at when obtaining customers. What does it cost to obtain the customer? That is called the Cost Per Order (CPO). What is your Average Lifetime Revenue Value (ALRV), or Average Order Value (AOV)? The cost to obtain the customer obviously has to be less than the cost you are going to receive in income from the customer. The bottom line in obtaining customers: you have to set up a system. You have to set up testing. You have to set up as many sources for obtaining customers as possible. Even though I was in the TV business, I didn't just get customers through TV. Customers came through TV, radio, the internet, retail stores, international distribution, home shopping channels, etc. The first step is to make a laundry list of every possible resource for attracting these customers.

Today, some people who are into the digital space are basically just getting customers on the internet. Some of the areas I mentioned above have become very expensive. It's tougher to make money on TV. While we started on TV, the cost to get customers has become too high; so we now have made the switch to digital. When you talk about internet, there's many different ways to obtain customers, from Google AdWords to Facebook ads to social media, etc. You can also attain customers with public relations and influencers. You have to decide what works best with your product. The bottom line is a lot of people do not realize they have to be sophisticated, from a business analysis standpoint, to set up a business. You need a marketing plan to obtain customers.

First, focus on two numbers: your Customer Acquisition Cost (CAT) and Average Order Value (AOV). Those numbers have to work. Customer service is crucial in the business world as well. A business can't have bad customer service and retain customers This is especially true in this day-and-age.

Raising Capital

I had a 50-million-dollar-a-year business, making $5 million a year in profit. Feeling confident, I met with seven banks to get some financing. I thought it was going to be easy because I had a very profitable business. Unfortunately, bank after bank after bank turned me down. I had great credit and all of that. The only asset I had was the business. Part of the problem was I didn't know how to approach the banks. I was a young entrepreneur in my twenties. I had no real credibility in the banking world; I was walking in and just showing my numbers from the year before.

So, what did I do to get the capital? Well, I ran into a mentor who was a former bank president, and he said, "Kevin, you went about it all wrong. I come from the banking business, and if you walked into my office and said, 'I need 5 million bucks,' I would have told you to turn around and get the hell out of my office. What do you have to do? You have to sell them on the future. What you did last year is well and good, but they are giving you money because they know that you are still going to be in business three years from now repaying their loans. You need projections. You need your forward business plan. You need your five-year master plan. You need to talk the talk and walk the walk, otherwise they aren't even interested."

I hired my mentor as a consultant to the company. I brought him in on the ground floor as part of my dream team. To make a long story short, we went back to re-pitch some of the same banks. We didn't get 5 million dollars, but we got a 3-million-dollar line of credit. It was all in how we talked to the banks. We had the same business, but it was all in the presentation. It's all in how you talk and how prepared you are. Raising capital is mental. It's in the pitch. It's in the relationships you build, etc.

One of the biggest challenges with any business is having enough capital to do the things you want to do. You have to have a successful business plan if you want to raise money. Here are the elements of a successful business plan.

(1) You need an executive summary (one page summarizing the whole plan). You need an industry overview, defining the problem you are solving and an overview of the market.

(2) You need a description of your product or the service. How does it serve as a solution?

(3) You need a competitive analysis. What/who is your competition?

(4) You need a sales and marketing plan.

(5) You need to identify your target customer and proof for your concept.

(6) What is your method of operations?

(7) Who's on your management team, your board of advisers, your dream team?

(8) What are your financial projections?

(9) You need to outline your risk analysis and appendix.

If you are going to raise capital, you don't just talk to an investor. I get people all the time that come to me saying they have an idea, and boom… it's on a napkin. They tell me that they just need $100K for 10 percent. I ask if they can send me their business plan. They then ask me what I mean when I say, 'business plan.' If they don't have one, that means I am going to end up giving them 100K and never see it again.

One of the most important parts of raising capital is coming up with a reasonable ask, and then explaining how the proceeds will be used. Many entrepreneurs don't understand this. For example, a guy came on *Shark Tank* saying he needed 150K for 10 percent of his company. I asked what he was going to use the 150K for?

His response was essentially this, "Well, I am going to use the money as a down payment for a piece of real estate where we are going to build a building, then launch the business."

"Okay, so you are going to build the building and then equip the building with furniture. Where is that money going to come from?" I asked. He said once he got the real estate, then they would figure out that batch of money at that time. I told him, "$150K dollars doesn't get you in business. $150K dollars gets you a piece of land. How are you going to build the business, generate revenue, and pay me back?" This guy told me he thought I would have more money for him after that. I said, "Well, no. You are not going to get the first batch of money based on the answers you are giving me."

Instead, he should have said he was going to lease a small office and start generating massive amounts of revenue with the money I gave them. Then, pay me back all of my money, plus a huge return on my investment, and then build it into a global business. That's what I wanted to hear. I want to know that people have a successful business plan, a successful marketing plan, and then I will talk about how to go about raising the capital, how to call on investors, and what the sweet spots are for the investors.

The bottom line on raising capital is, you can't just go build yourself a huge global business without thinking about how you're going to finance it. In the old days, I thought if I built a successful business, money was going to be easy. It's not, unless you know how to do it. There's an art to raising capital. Part of it involves making sure you are prepared and know how to pitch your business properly.

The Perfect Pitch

While the actual product or service you are trying to sell is a critical part of the process, it is just as important to sell the customer on yourself, your services, and your business. Even though I have made thousands upon thousands of pitches, have spoken to thousands of people, and have seen a great amount of success, I still pitch myself and my businesses. No matter who you are, or what you do, you have to be ready to drop the perfect pitch. It doesn't matter if you are going to make this perfect pitch in front of a crowd of thousands, or a crowd of one. To help with the concept of a perfect pitch, I have created a 10-step system.

Before you can start perfecting the perfect pitch, you have to ask yourself a couple of questions. What are you pitching? In other words, what product, business, or service are you trying to sell? Next, what do you want to get out of this pitch? More customers? More sales? Nonetheless, these questions are for you to answer, and you need to answer them before devising your perfect pitch. The perfect pitch can be broken down into these 10 steps:

(1) The **Tease** is your hook; the period of time when you plant the seed. This is when you reveal a problem. You have to explain to your customers why you are giving the pitch. You also have to use showmanship, which sets the pace for the rest of the pitch. If your showmanship skills are demonstrated in the Tease portion of your pitch, then you will have your audience (or your customer) hooked from the very beginning.

(2) Next up is **Please**. In this part of the perfect pitch, you are telling your customer how your product or service can solve the problem you mapped out in the first step. Ideally, your product or service will solve this stated problem in the most efficient, elegant, and cost-effective way. You have to relay to your customer that your solution is the best solution, and it will solve the problem better than anything (or anyone) else. It is important to also show off your features and benefits, and to display the magical transformation that will take place.

(3) The third step to the perfect pitch is **Demonstration/Multi-functionality**. First, you have to ask yourself if you can demonstrate your product, your service and your value. This is the key to any successful pitch, and it brings multi-functionality to the forefront. It shows it off. Think of this step as an added value. Ideally, your service or product is multifunctional. If you can show this off to your customer, then you just brought bonus points to the table.

(4) But Wait There's More! is the fourth step, and it's not just for infomercials on TV. This is the step where you give more value to your product or service by showing and adding more to the pitch—maybe added bonus items or "buy 2 get 1 free if you act now" incentives. At this point, your customer should already be biting, but now is the time to really win them over. So, show them what else you have to offer.

(5) Testimonials are the fifth step to creating the perfect pitch. You are now using someone else to do the pitching. In other words, who says so besides you? This is the proof behind your business, product, or service. Testimonials can include consumers (actual users of the product or service), professionals (leaders in your industry), editorial (articles, experts, press, journals, trade publications, magazines, newspapers), etc. Testimonials can also feature celebrities. Celebrity testimonials can be very powerful for the simple fact that people love celebrities. Then there are documented testimonials, which can include clinical studies, labs tests, and science. Once again, this is one of the most important areas for creating the perfect pitch.

(6) Another important step is **Research and Competitive Analysis**. For this step, you should be asking yourself if you have done your research. If so, then this is the portion of the perfect pitch when you show off all of that information. This can include information on the industry, market and competitors. It can also be facts, figures, and statistics. This research should show off the fact that you, your company, and your product/service is unique.

(7) The seventh step is **Your Team.** In this step, you are bringing the credibility of your team and putting it right there on the metaphorical table. Who makes up your team? It could be advisers, management, directors, and strategic partners. Your team will help scale, open connections, add on the knowledge factor, and so much more.

(8) Why? is the eighth step. Why are you pitching? How will the person in front of you help? This step will change based on who you are actually pitching to. For example, if you are looking for funds, then this is a big section, and you need to incorporate many talking points.

(9) The ninth step is **Marketing Plan.** You have done your pitch and given out all your information. Now, how will you make everything happen? For instance, you need to know your marketing and distribution plan. As is the case throughout your entire pitch, it is essential that you show confidence. Sell whoever you are pitching on your product or service, and yourself as well. People invest in people all the time.

(10) The 10th and final step is **Seize**. You laid everything out, now ask! What are you trying to accomplish? Ask it! Being the final step, this is the time to present the final call to action.

Remember, each pitch will be different. Some pitches last for over an hour and others last only a few seconds or minutes. It just depends on how much time you are given or how much time you need. That is why you need to craft your pitches accordingly. Practice, practice, and more practice.

***

To contact Kevin:

www.KevinHarrington.tv

Shenal Arimilli

Shenal is passionate about her mission to empower millions as she masterfully merges the power of science with the age-old wisdom of consciousness to create quantum leaps in transforming lives, businesses and consciousness worldwide!

As a transformational leader, motivational speaker, mentor, author, and workshop facilitator in life transformation, she teaches powerful techniques to create profound shifts. As a thought leader and visionary, she pushes the envelope for change and leads people to be powerful beyond measure.

While Shenal's degrees from the University of California at Berkeley and Chapman University created a valuable educational background, she believes that what she learned through her life's journey is invaluable.

Her personal story of healing through cancer and its recurrences, led her to a deeper understanding of quantum physics, neuroscience, physiology, psychology, and spirituality as it relates to our power to change. Shenal's signature approach and intuitive understanding of what is needed to elevate lives and businesses makes her a celebrated speaker, workshop facilitator and private mentor.

She is a featured speaker on Amazon Prime's Show, SpeakUP, Season 3, Episode 2. Her life-changing work is recognized on major media outlets, international stages, radio shows, podcasts, and in BW Business World Magazine. Her awards include *Exceptional Woman of Excellence* at the International Women's Economic Forum.

She is grateful for her amazing husband of 28+ years, her 2 beautiful young adult children, her clients who inspire her and the magic and miracles of life itself!

Unlock Your Treasure Chest

By Shenal Arimilli

"The greatest treasure you will ever discover is the one that lies within you. Unlock this and you will find the power to change and create YOUR RICH LIFE!"~ Shenal

What if *you* are more *powerful* than you may know in this moment? What if there is something magnificent within you that is waiting to be met?

For those who are driven to evolve from the "inside-out", their inner leader, their innate power, their ability to *co-create miracles* and ultimately, their right to live a fully RICH life will be met!

What would it feel like to live this fully RICH life? How do we even go about creating that?

My Story From Corporate Leader to Change Maker

Early in my career, I was incredibly fortunate to land beside a CEO who saw something in me. Under his wings, I went from Director of Rehabilitation at our hospital to securing a senior position in Healthcare Management and Administration for two hospitals, making a hefty sum of money early in life.

But something was missing. I just was not aware enough then to know what that was. Let's fast forward some years to when I chose a brief career as a stay-at-home mom before I co-founded a company in the fashion industry. Both of these experiences were rewarding and humbling. My first go at entrepreneurship went from visibility and glamour to losing lots of money but learning a lot about business. But what I still had not understood, was life itself.

But as life would have it, it must have been time for me to learn what I may have been putting off far too long. In my seemingly "perfect" life I received a dreadful phone call. "Shenal, you have cancer." I had no idea that this wake-up call was the beginning of my *great awakening.*

For me, it was this challenge of healing through cancer and its recurrences that made me pause and begin to seek the truth about myself and this life. It pushed me to gain more from this life than I had scratched at the surface.

I dug deep into the physical and spiritual laws of the Universe and how they impact our life here on Earth. I dug even deeper within myself and began peeling away the layers of falsehood that I had been living, mostly unconsciously. I met the limiting beliefs I had been handed down from my ancestors and those learned along the way. I processed the emotions buried within due to pain or distractions in life. I began resolving past traumas that had been left dismissed and unresolved. I faced the survival mechanisms employed in order to feel safe, loved, accepted, and valued and the many misunderstood concepts of who I am and what this life is really all about. This was my "inside" job.

What unfolded through this journey is what led me to my passion, my purpose and my life's work! Using a deeply intuitive yet firmly scientifically grounded process to help people create quantum leaps in transforming lives personally, professionally and spiritually, I knew I had found my calling! This is my "outside" job.

My Life's Work

There are three I's that propel me forward on my mission.

Inspiration: waking each day feeling inspired to do my life's work.

Impact: trusting that what drives me is making a positive difference in lives around the world.

Income: receiving with gratitude as the more I have, the more I can enjoy the gift of this life and the more I can give back and serve humanity.

I learned that I had been living a partially RICH life, not a fully RICH life. My new-found definition and five pillars of living a fully RICH life now include:
  o *inner peace*
  o *true love*
  o *immense joy*
  o *vibrant health*
  o *financial wealth*

One aspect of the RICH life without the other feels incomplete. When all of these components are fully nurtured and energetically aligned in our lives, the RICH life is not only touched but fully lived!

What I understand through my journey is that based on the law of resonance, vibration and attraction, our life and our business is a reflection of what lives within us. Turning our lives and businesses around is an *INSIDE-OUT job*! When we take personal responsibility to create our personal reality, we are essentially stepping into our power as a creator.

> *"Everything is energy and that's all there is to it. Match the frequency of the reality you want, and you cannot help but get that reality. It can be no other way. This is not philosophy. This is physics."~ Albert Einstein*

Our soul too, is seeking this deeply RICH experience in life – one where we understand who we truly are and what we are capable of – one where we learn to live with inner peace, experience the true essence of love, find joy in even the simplest of things, abound with vibrant health, and receive the abundance of financial wealth! This is living a fully RICH life.

From research, book knowledge, and Divine Wisdom available to all (that Wisdom that came well before the books of knowledge were even written), I have come to realize how both science and spirituality are pointing us in the direction of our capacity to change and ultimately become powerful co-creators of our miracles – living that fully RICH life!

Whether that miracle to be created is around health, love, career, or money, I have learned that the process is the same. I distilled down a 3 step A.T.M. Process to Creating and Living an Abundant Life™ that includes, *Awakening, Transforming, and Manifesting*. Regardless of what challenge or opportunity pushes us to seek more out of life, the "how" is the same.

Let us use the example of career and finance. If you are looking to accelerate your career, quadruple your income, launch or scale up your business, or align with your life's work, here are *six keys* that I have successfully used in helping leaders, mentors, coaches, seekers and small businesses to unlock and remove deeply buried internal blocks and align with success!

6 Keys to Unlock Your Treasure Chest

Master Key 1: Tending to Your Life's Garden

While having a positive mindset and uplifted emotions are crucial for the unfolding of a RICH life, having the courage to meet our underlying beliefs, past programming, and buried emotions is a vital part of creating a true shift.

Take a garden for example. Would you plant seeds of flowers in a bed of weeds? I did try this early in my journey with positive affirmations and gratitude journaling, but I did not heal. It was when I cleared away the layers of limiting beliefs, survival programming, buried emotions, and unresolved traumas (the weeds in my garden), that I could make way for the new mindset, positive emotions, and inspired actions to actually flourish into the life that I am grateful to be living now.

Tip: Tend to the weeds in your garden by having the courage to meet what lives inside of you – the negative thoughts, beliefs, emotions, and traumas. Use journaling as one process to allow what is buried to be brought into the light. Then FEEL what it would be like to shift that to something positive. This is the sowing of the seeds, elevating of consciousness and raising your vibration for a new experience.

Master Key 2: Healing Your Money and Success Relationship

Did you know that we have a relationship with everything in life? That includes other people, the Creative Intelligence in the Universe, yourself, your body, and yes, MONEY! Wouldn't it serve us well then to heal this relationship in order to have a healthier financial outcome?

Our relationships with money and success are often handed down from generations past, learned from our parents and caretakers, or accepted and memorized from our past failures or traumas. From the perspective of neuroscience, we "learn and memorize" these much like the ABC's which then become a part of our subconscious programming. This programming then creates a "relationship" with money and success which will be either healthy or unhealthy.

I had to dig deep to heal this relationship and align with money and success myself. I can share two significant pieces I had to bring into my conscious awareness to shift in order for me to experience greater success and increased money flow.

I heard stories growing up about how my grandfather in the 1800's travelled by ship from India to London to study textiles at Oxford University. Quite an accomplishment back then. Bringing the first corduroy to India, he soon became a prominent businessman, revered by many. The stories of him being picked up by horse and carriage at their bungalow daily to be taken to his textile plant and showered with gifts and treasures from people all around India, colored my childhood mind. Little did I know that he gave up EVERYTHING and went from riches to rags in a spiritual pursuit, believing that wealth was not spiritual.

When I struggled myself to accept payment for sharing my intuitive gifts – for helping people heal themselves, turning their relationships around, and even build their bank accounts, I had to face this ancestral pattern that was unconsciously holding me back. I had to lovingly accept my ancestor's choices while choosing differently, embracing for myself that having wealth without greed and attachment can serve humanity immensely while supporting my spiritual life.

Also playing out in my subconscious was my mother's voice repeatedly sharing with me that the pursuit of money will destroy the family life. I had not realized that my success was being unconsciously limited by someone else's understanding and belief system. For me I had to rewrite that story in my heart and mind to see success as something that comes with balance, serves the family, and even offers a financial freedom that allows for MORE family time!

Tip: Set aside some time to reflect back on what you had heard about your ancestors and also what you "observed" and eventually "learned" about money and success growing up. Also take time to understand how your own past experiences may have set into motion a relationship with fear, lack or impossibility around success and financial freedom. In the light of your awareness, you have the power to shift the energy rather than fighting against it unconsciously!

Master Key 3: Opening to Receive and Balancing Giving and Receiving

Nature has a phenomenal way of teaching us how we are intended to live life. Every breath we take is a reminder that we must balance *giving and receiving*. Just exhaling and *giving* CO_2 to our planet without inhaling, would leave us lifeless. And just breathing in and *receiving* O_2 without exhaling, would leave us toxic and again lifeless. Balance is required.

As a recovering people-pleaser, I have had to learn how to *receive*. Unfortunately, and fortunately, it took cancer to help me to break that pattern. The energy and vibration of receiving opens us to receive all that the Universe has available to us including support, resources, love, healing, success, and money!

Tip: Release all limiting beliefs that receiving is somehow bad, weak, selfish, greedy, needy or the likes. Choose to give, but not over-give in order to be loved and valued. Balancing *giving* and *receiving* is key. Allow yourself the permission to align with RECEIVING.

Master Key 4: Moving From Surviving to Creating

Whether you are an entrepreneur in a start-up or running a business, from the top down, the fear of not "making it" keeps us in survival and out of our full capacity to create. Just imagine, survival is like having a tiger in the room. Here, the neurochemistry in our body keeps us running, fighting or hiding to survive. Perceiving that there is a tiger in the room will NOT interest us in any sort of creative energy, but rather, protective, survival-like energy. It is a brilliant innate survival mechanism when actual threat exists, but unfortunately, we see much of our life and business like a tiger. In survival we diminish or eliminate our creative power to learn, build, and grow a thriving business.

Survival mechanisms are born from fear, threat and danger. Those fears may include lack, failure, and even at the deepest level, separation from the Source of Creative Intelligence in the Universe. When we stop living and running our business as if there is a tiger in the room, our brain can perceive safety and allow us to access our creative power to take our life and business to a whole new level.

Tip: One of the most powerful ways to communicate with the brain to create shifts out of survival is breath work. Take time throughout the day, to pause, breathe deeply and slowly. We would never breathe this way if a tiger was in the room, so doing this will message the brain that you are safe, allowing blood supply to return to your core and to your creative, intelligent brain, rather than your primitive survival brain. Breath work taps into our brain's neuroplasticity and helps create new patterns.

Master Key 5: The Courage to Move Out of Your Comfort Zone

Once again, nature reflects back to us the way of life. For example, the birthing canal represents to us our innate capacity to move through contractions, darkness, uncertainty, and the discomfort which comes when we are birthing something new and bringing life to something special. Your life, business and career also move through this process.

It is truly through this process where new things can be born. It does not mean that we must have NO fear to move out of our comfort zone. It simply means that we must fear less, trust more, and step out of our comfort zone to reach new heights.

Tip: Fear is a part of our human journey, yet when faced, it no longer runs our life. So first, spend time writing down your fears…fear of failure, success, what people will think, of not having a family life, of not being spiritual, etc.

Meet it, greet it, release it, and replace it! Don't ignore it as these beliefs and fears are seeking to come into the light where they can shift.

Awareness is huge. *Action* is important. But when BOTH are combined, amazing results happen! Become aware of what lives within you around money and success. Then have the courage to identify small, inspired actions that may push you out of your comfort zone. Remember, this is what will set you in motion towards greater success and financial freedom!

Master Key 6: Access Your Power to Change and Create

Many teach mindset shifts. Others focus on emotional intelligence. And yet others will coach on goal setting and action. I work with all three simultaneously to help you to exercise your power to manage your *thoughts, emotions and actions* and ultimately influence the way your life unfolds. We then align with our role here as a co-creator of our life, elevating our consciousness, vibration, and ultimately, our life and our business!

This is the *Cup of T.E.A.*™ process that I have been using successfully. We must reach for our old *Cup of T.E.A.* ™ first and assess our **T**houghts, **E**motions, and **A**ctions that have been driving our current circumstances in life or in business. Then we must reach for a new *Cup of T.E.A.* ™ and create **T**houghts, **E**motions, and **A**ctions aligned with our conscious creation of a new reality.

T = Thoughts: When our thoughts are repeated, they lead to beliefs. Beliefs that we carry, lead to patterns in our life. Some patterns serve us well while others are limiting. To create a shift, we must become keenly aware of our thoughts, stop them, and then shift them.

E = Emotions: Our ability to feel is what makes us human. The whole spectrum of emotions is important for us to honor. E-motions, "energy in motion", are intended to be acknowledged, not repressed. Whether it is the feeling of fear, worry, shame or doubt, when we honor them, we have the ability to heal them. Keep in mind, feeling is healing. The next step is to reach for a higher emotion that we can feel which will create the shift through the principle of entrainment.

A = Actions – We have the *power* to choose our actions. Like emotions that cover a spectrum, I have identified a spectrum of ACTIONS.

InACTION <----> **Inspired ACTION** <----> DistrACTION

InAction is at one end of the spectrum. Here we feel stuck, unmotivated and stagnant. Don't mistake this for those quiet moments where we are waiting for the inspiration. That is different. Inaction keeps us in a "comfort zone" of doing nothing.

DistrAction is at the other end of the spectrum. This is "busy" work where we feel overwhelmed, overworked, and not focused yet busy.

This busy work unconsciously distracts us and keeps us from getting out of our comfort zone and making needed changes.

Inspired Action is the balance point where we get the most out of our input. Here we feel aligned with our intentions, goals, and dreams. Our efforts do not feel like "hard work" or "struggle" but rather flow.

Tip: The *CUP OF T.E.A.*™ process will help you to change and create a new reality. Remember, what you think, feel and do are in your *power* so choose wisely! This can make the difference between a dream and a reality!

> *"Change your THOUGHTS. Change your EMOTIONS. Change your ACTIONS. Change your LIFE!* ~ Shenal

If I Can. If They Can. You Can!

Let me share just the tip of the iceberg of what is possible. Let's be inspired by real life successes from my clients around the world.

Quadrupled Income – CFO making ~ \$250K came needing to heal a repeated personal relationship pattern but by removing internal roadblocks, took his salary to just shy of \$1 M within a year.

Mid-size Start-up Multiplies Sales by Millions – An all-hands workshop with co-founders and staff led to breaking free of the start-up survival mindset to create an opening for greater expansion and financial wins!

Slow Business to Booming Business – Working to help the co-owners of a branding company to align their energies to success individually and collectively resulted in their client base multiplying.

Increased Clients – Numerous solopreneurs have reported gains in their private client base even the day of or day after a private session as they break free of limiting beliefs and unresolved ancestral patterns in relationship to money and/or success.

Alignment with Passion, Purpose and Their Life's Work – Clients who are searching for their purpose, afraid to follow their dreams, or not sure how to listen to their inner calling, have found new career opportunities and gained certifications in different arenas of work from their currently held positions by releasing belief systems around the pursuit of one's soul's gifts and heart's desires.

My Message to You

We all have the capacity to live a fully RICH life. When we change what lies within us, we step into our power to create a better life and thriving business. Doing this work from the "inside out" allows us to release energetic resistance and open the channels for flow of resources, ideas, people, success and financial gains to move towards us.

Coming into an alignment creates an inner receptivity that brings more of what we really want to create into reality. I have seen for myself and countless others what is possible when we shift what lies within us. I have witnessed countless miracles.

There is a treasure chest within you waiting to be opened. Fortunately, we were born with the keys. They are in our hands. The choice to use them is ours!

My invitation to you is to unlock the power that lies within *you* to create and live the fully RICH life! It is waiting for *you*!

***

To Contact Shenal:

Email: Shenal@ShenalArimilli.com

To Book Shenal as a Speaker or Workshop Facilitator

http://www.shenalarimilli.com/speaking/

To Book a Complimentary 1:1 Discovery Session - Breakthrough a Barrier and Receive a Roadmap to Elevate Your Life and Business

http://www.shenalarimilli.com/contact-2/

To Watch Shenal on Amazon Prime if you are WITHIN the USA and UK

https://www.amazon.com/gp/video/detail/B0949DKB88/ref=atv_d p_share_cu_r?mc_cid=e9d965de3c&mc_eid=a5977c362e

To Watch Shenal on Amazon Prime if you are OUTSIDE of the USA and UK

https://www.mpn.global/speakup-episodes-3?mc_cid=e9d965de3c&mc_eid=a5977c362e

For General Inquires

www.ShenalArimilli.com

To Download Your Complimentary Copy of her latest eBook, Elevate Your Life: 7 Keys to Unlock the Power Within Your

http://www.shenalarimilli.com/get-your-free-ebook/

To Speak Directly

Phone: 925-575-7699

Social Media

LinkedIn

https://www.linkedin.com/in/shenal-arimilli-mpt-03692254/

Youtube Channel

https://www.youtube.com/channel/UCAt9rl8kF7g7aM-VNNkMj7Q

Facebook

https://www.facebook.com/CoCreateYourMiracles

Amy Bolding

Amy Bolding is an international Les Brown certified speaker, author, awareness coach, and founder of The Pickled Heart, LLC. She lives firmly by her trademarked slogan, "I CAN, I WILL, I'M WORTH IT!" She has over 20 years of proven leadership in the sales and healthcare industries and believes the key to any longstanding success is mindset. That success is not about where you come from or who you are, but about starting from where you are, and believing you can! Amy has great passion for helping people reach their highest potential. She caters to clients from Los Angeles all the way to the Netherlands. Her philosophy is that we all have something to give, but we must first believe we are worth it. Her writings influence those who may feel less than qualified to live a life of wealth. She believes, we all have work to do, nobody is ever finished, as learning is a lifelong deal, but it's how we live it that makes all the difference.

Being Beyond Good

By Amy Bolding

In this chapter I will share personal stories about strategy and mindset when it comes to people and bottom lines. My hope is that sharing this information will get you beyond being, just "good." Spending over 20 years of my life in management, I have grown in many ways. I have led virtual teams, opened franchises, handled a staff of over 200, and consulted across the states just to name a few. The information I have to offer will help you regardless of your business or position. Perhaps you are an owner of a company, part of a leadership team, a CEO or COO, no matter the position, I am sure you will get something from this chapter. I am happy to say I now do what I truly love, and all my experiences have been an asset to who I am, and what I do now.

Many things have changed for people since the pandemic, and they did for me too. The last 10 years of my management was in healthcare, I was there to see many lives taken day after day. A person can only see so much death before they start to think about their own life. It didn't take long before I took a step back to reevaluate how I wanted to spend the next season of my life. So I leaped, and here I am, writing this chapter.

The Entrepreneur

From an entrepreneurial perspective, you'll have to learn to get over yourself. In order to go further than you have ever gone, you have to believe bigger than you have ever believed. You cannot simply say you're going to build this million-dollar idea with a five-dollar level of belief. It has been said that the richest place in the world is the graveyard, because so many million-dollar ideas went to the grave with people without ever being expressed. How does that happen? It happens because people are afraid they are not worthy of their dream. They're afraid that their idea will be rejected, laughed at, and a waste of time. Or that they will fail publicly and that it will shatter their reputation. Failing is a beautiful thing because it means you are trying. My acronym for FAIL is F- Finding, A-Another, I-Intentional L-Lesson. If you have the courage to take steps towards your dreams, you're bound to find several opportunities to F.A.I.L. in the process.

Self-confidence is everything. I really had to wrap my head around this one. I didn't understand what "self-confidence" was. I had heard it but didn't quite understand how to get it. I soon realized that if you aren't confident in who you are, you will cower at anything you didn't know how to do, or that you wouldn't try unfamiliar things because you lacked the confidence. Self-confidence says, I CAN, I WILL, I'M WORTH IT! No matter what it is! That I don't have to come from a particular background or family, and I didn't have to possess a bunch of degrees, that I can have whatever I set my mind to, as long as I have the self-confidence to believe it and pursue it. If you don't believe in yourself, you can't expect anybody else to either. The issue is we get in our own way with our clouded thinking. We think riches are for a select few, and we don't believe it is possible for the average person. That stems from a self-esteem problem, not a shortage of riches and opportunities in the world problem. The world is the greatest recycling center of wealth and abundance. You just have to believe you are worthy enough of having a slice of that pie!

Keeping Secrets

Sometimes your idea is best to be kept secret, if you come from an environment like I did, you'd understand that telling anyone about some lofty dream would be reason for a total mockery. Here is the thing, the dream you see, the vision you have, the inspiration you feel when you think of your idea, that is your golden ticket. Sad to say, but there are people who will tell you more reasons why you can't do something than reasons why you can. You can't afford to let doubt enter your mind. Once you see it, go study it, go find out more, go chase it and start acting on it. ACTION, ACTION, ACTION. The "how" will appear along the way, you just have to believe enough to act on it. It might be that your final destination isn't what you initially started out after, but the lesson or road along the way to it may lead you to the million-dollar idea. What I can guarantee you is, to get to it, you have to get started. You will have to make moves on inspiration, you have to follow through, and you have to be consistent, and disciplined. So, remember, you don't need to look for approval for your ideas and thoughts.

I understand you want someone to be just as excited about your endeavor as you are, but until you start to get around the like-minded, you will probably be best keeping it to yourself. Sometimes your hardest critics are the ones you love. You have to remember no matter how many people come along on your journey to becoming, mentors, coaches, influences, and people, this idea, this creation, this purpose you are living and expressing is an inside job. It is your baby, literally. It is your job to take it from a thought (conception), and train it up to walk on its own. It's your job to push it out. Mentors, coaches, are necessary to keep you on track because it takes a village to raise a child. There is an African Proverb that says, "If you want to go fast, go alone, but if you want to go far, go together." That is so important because you will need guides along the way to help you go farther. Reaching success is not done alone. There is not one project completed that didn't depend on a resource outside of the one creating the project. Until you find those who are appointed along your path, keep it to yourself.

Another point of reality when aiming for the moon in life, is to realize there will be many moments when you are paddling alone, just you and your dream (you will feel it from time to time while looking at FB or Instagram and seeing photos of everyone having a good time, while you are eating a peanut butter sandwich and drinking ice water out of a wine glass trying to stay inspired to keep climbing this steep hill to get to those dreams). I wish I could tell you that simply thinking about how things will be in 5 years will make you feel better, but it wouldn't be the truth. This is where a lot of entrepreneurs quit, because they would rather give up their dream than to feel lonely. Your mind has to be well disciplined, should you abandon your dream for anything, it will always haunt you. Be willing to say no to the things that pull you away from what matters.

Sales and Management

Employees are very important to your business. If you were to ask me what brought me success in all my leadership and management roles, I would say, understanding how to treat people. How was I able to reduce overtime, create better bottom lines, break company records, have great staff retention, reduce turnovers, and reduce state deficiencies? It was all about listening and being a part of what was going on. I didn't manage from up top in the glass office, I was on the floor where things either broke records, or broke budgets. Stay on the inside. Let's look at it in terms of basketball. If you guard the inside well, any shot taken is forced so far out, they generally miss the shot. You didn't leave a hole to the basket, you defended well. That's how I look at leadership and management. If you understand the game (career) you know what is valuable. Generally, it's the bottom line, as we know if it doesn't make money, it doesn't make business, which doesn't make sense.

As a manager/owner/entrepreneur, you can't manage by a monthly projection sheet, by then it is too late. It has to be looked at daily. To correct a score card of production at a monthly glance, you are 30 days behind correcting a problem. Daily stats, daily results. Be personable. I would tell the employees as they were coming in, good morning, and when they left, I told them have a great day. Prior to the morning shift starting, I was filling them up with positive words, and honest expectations. If there was a tough customer concern, or an irate family member, I didn't run from them, or leave it for the employees to figure out, I would go help. Be there for your employees, let them see your face.

As an owner of a company, you need to seek this type of management. No matter how beautifully you sign your name to that paycheck, it's the management that pushes the employees everyday which leads you to a better financial success. Training is crucial. No matter the business, no matter the price, training is everything. With proper training, your sales team feels more confident, and it will show. Teach technique, teach etiquette. How good does it feel when you reach a great customer service experience? It feels great right? I have personally paid more for something because of the person behind the product. Your staff will only represent what you as a company have invested in them. If they feel powerless selling or introducing your product, they will cower at the first obstacle. Get a trainer with enthusiasm, commitment, and keep on going training. Nobody gets it all in orientation.

Know what is important to your staff. The reason this is important is finding out what will incentivize them. Ask your staff for ideas. They will feel great giving their input, and if you should choose to use something they say, they'll feel included. One year, the company I was managing sent a box of "things" for staff appreciation. They were all picked out by the marketing team. Here is the thing, the marketing team is there to help sell the business to potential clients, the staff is there to keep the business alive. Two different groups of people. A staff member wants to be thanked, thought of, and appreciated. Not wooed by ink pens with the company name on it. Take pride in staff appreciation. I know plenty of people who stayed with me in my years of being with a company simply because they felt appreciated, even when other places were paying more. True gratitude goes a long way. People give up 60% of their day at work, and at times companies stick with mandatory overtime. My point is this: People matter. Your employees can take your company somewhere you can't take it alone. Never forget that. Don't take shortcuts, do the right thing. Treat people like you care, and they will take care of you.

Weed the garden. A lot of companies let bad apples stay around and make the workplace a negative environment, while hoping they'll quit. Bad move. Every day you avoid properly addressing an employee who is creating a bad workplace environment is a day you lost something, usually money. Keep a good paper trail, use creative discussion methods, and see if you can help get to a positive solution, but it must be addressed. Don't be afraid to have hard conversations. Do not wait for problems to correct themselves. Time is money.

Creating the vision

Have a vision for your company so big that you have no clue how to achieve it. People and companies have their own set of rules when it comes to goal setting, I do too. If you can do the very thing you are reaching for with no help, no faith, no questions, and no how will I ever get this done questions, it's not a goal, it's a given. Aim big! When we leap into our vision, we first see it in its full picture and potential, then over time we start trimming away at the parts we don't know how we would be able to do. For instance, maybe you envisioned your company bringing in a million for the year, but then you second guess yourself. You start to look around at your current situation and say, "Well how can I do that when I only have this?" So instead of starting and believing, you start trimming down the goal. So now instead of you holding a goal of a million you switch it to a goal of 25K and find a reason to justify it. Don't do that, reach for that million dollar a year goal, and guess what, if you didn't reach it, oh well, you keep at it. Do not water down your goal. Every time you do that you are taking from yourself, robbing your potential with your own hands! You are worth your desires, but you have to believe in them. You have to believe in the process and allow room for great things to happen. You are not supposed to know every single detail. That is one of the most enjoyable parts for those who believe, but one of the most stressful parts for those who have little faith. You will meet great opportunities with preparation, but don't think for one second that even with the greatest of preparation that you won't meet adversity, because you will. Don't look at the scorecard of the how vs. what, and just keep pushing ahead.

Aim to be you. So many people want to be like other millionaires or billionaires. I repeat, aim to be you. Please understand you will, and you should, learn from those in your field, but not to be them, to learn from them. They are already taken, you're all you got, be you. If you go into business to be like someone, you will be miserable. You will be looking to fulfill yourself with someone else's happiness. It never works. So, no matter what you do, always remember you are you, not them. How many times have you heard the story of the son who was told to be like his father and he grew to hate his life even when he made a great deal of success and money? There is enough money to go around, this universe is the greatest recycling center there is. Money goes in and around quicker than ever, it is literally at your fingertips. So why not make the money doing what you love, while being you!

Knowing what is important

Never forget the things that are important. I ran myself thin for companies for years. Yes the paychecks and quarterly bonuses were sweet, and I had vacation time to boot! But guess what, I couldn't use the vacation time because the work was too demanding. As far as the money, it ended up substituting quality time with my kids. After some years of this, I said no more. I was going to take vacations, I was going to go home on time, and I was going to remember what was truly important. Please understand, success will take hard work and long hours, but with a disciplined use of time, you can win at spending time where it matters most.

One of the reasons this is so important is because no matter how many times we say our personal life doesn't affect our career life, it is far from the truth. Stress at home shows up in our work. Just like stress at work will show up in our home. Find balance, it matters not just to your health, but to your bottom line as well. You have to be good to yourself, or you will end up falling apart, and so will everything you worked so hard for. It is best said this way, if you don't make time for your wellness, you'll be forced to take time for your illness. The choice is yours.

Flexibility

No matter what you learn, what you choose, what you do, be flexible. You may spend 10 years on one thing and find out that it is not what you are going to be doing anymore. You may change careers many times in your life, and that's ok. You may start a business that lands you bankrupt, more than once, and that too, is ok. You may have to change your entire business model, and that's ok. You may have to move across the states, and start all over in an unfamiliar area, and that's ok, too. This needs to be your attitude in life and in entrepreneurship. One of my own quotes is, be careful cementing your feet, because you never know when you will have to change directions. Just know, everything will be ok. Stay flexible.

It all comes down to this:

Let's touch on all I mentioned here.

-Learn to get over yourself.

-Stay out of your own way and just create.

-Learn that to F.A.I.L. is simply you F=finding A=another I=intentional L=lesson.

-Action, you must act on your inspiration. Start from where you are, don't doubt yourself. The steps will appear, just go!

-Treat your employees well. It will make all the difference in your bottom line. Be a part of your business in a real way. If you are an owner and have too much to do to be involved with day-to-day operations, hire a manager who is personable, and involved with the team.

-Training, quality training is vital to a business.

-Aim big, do not dummy down or dilute your aspirations.

-Keep it to yourself, until you find the like-minded.

-Make it your life mission to be the best "you" possible, it will reflect in all you do.

-Balance your life and be mindful of what matters, including your health.

-Experience life in the pursuit of your dreams. It is important to stay in touch with the things that are meaningful, natural, and inspiring.

-Be willing to learn, be willing to start over, and have the courage to never quit!

-You're worth it!

***

To contact Amy:

(619)770-9847

Website https://thepickledheart.com

Email thepickledheart@gmail.com

Facebook/AmyBolding

Instagram @ladybolding

Clubhouse @ladybolding

Andria Barrett

Andria Barrett is a Prediabetes Nutritionist & Wellness Expert. She teaches busy professionals and entrepreneurs how to lose weight and lower their blood sugar so they can beat Type 2 Diabetes.

A healthy body leads to a healthy business. A healthy business leads to a more profitable business.

Born and raised in Canada (with an allegiance to the Toronto Raptors), Andria is inspired by her own journey to overcome a family history of Type 2 Diabetes.

Andria believes there is a direct correlation between the food you eat, the supplements you take and the way you look and feel—which then translates to positive gains in your productivity and profitability.

She combines her knowledge of food with health and wellness. She's best known for giving clients the straight goods about what they need to stay on the right side of good health. She's committed to helping her clients learn how to balance their blood sugar to beat prediabetes. Andria teaches globally, sharing her tips and strategies for *kissing high blood sugar goodbye.*

Andria believes in the power of food and can teach you how to lower your blood sugar, one bite at a time.

She has been featured in several publications and is a regular expert on radio & TV.

Healthier Body, Healthier Business

By Andria Barrett

YOU'RE LEAVING MONEY ON THE TABLE

If you're like most high performers and entrepreneurs, your diet could probably use a little help. You're probably sleep deprived, dehydrated, stressed, a little overweight, have high blood sugar and not quite as healthy as you would like to be.

What's the point of being a top professional or entrepreneur if you're not healthy enough to enjoy it? Really. What's the point?

Believe it or not, taking care of your health is one of the best things you can do for your bottom line. Your body and brain run on fuel, and that fuel starts with the food and beverages you're putting into your body.

NUTRITION COULD BE THE MISSING LINK

By nutrition, I don't mean trendy, fad diets with exotic foods from far off places or foods that take hours to prepare in the kitchen.

Think about it. You are what you eat, remember? I like to think of it like this: your *business is as healthy as what you eat.* A bad diet is preventing you from maximizing sales and profits. You could be making more money. You work hard so your business can generate profits, serve clients and share your brilliance. But, what's the point if you're not well enough to enjoy it?

So many professionals and entrepreneur's workday and night to grow their businesses, only to neglect their health because they skip meals, don't get enough sleep, and seem to eat everything with sugar in it—if they're actually eating anything at all. That's a recipe for prediabetes.

I'm the prediabetes nutritionist who helps people lose weight and lower their blood sugar naturally, so they can have more energy, focus, mental clarity and grow the best business possible. My goal is to shift the outcomes for people with prediabetes.

I'M AT ALL-OUT WAR WITH DIABETES

All. Out. War.

First, it was my grandmother. Then, my mother, and then my father. Three people in my family diagnosed with Type 2 Diabetes. It felt like there was a bullseye on our family, and I was next.

As a little girl, I remember peeking into the bathroom to see my grandmother lift her shirt and stab herself in the side with an insulin needle. She would say, *"Andria, go get Granny's insulin. My needle is in the fridge."*

I also remember watching my mother lug along what looked like a second purse, just for her medication. Growing up, I didn't understand that there was a direct correlation between what you ate and its impact on your blood sugar—and therefore your health. Over time, I too started to get a little bigger, until one day the doctor looked at me at said, *"You need to lose a few pounds, or you're headed in the same direction as your mom and grandmother."* That was all it took.

I saw what they were going through and wanted nothing of it. You may not know you have prediabetes. You may have been told that you are overweight, and your blood sugar is too high. It's important to get tested, and then take steps to lose weight and lower your blood sugar.

I HAVE A SWEET TOOTH

I've never met a piece of dessert that I didn't like (except Black Forrest Cake—those fake cherries are not for me). So, what's a girl that loves dessert, and who needs to lose weight and lower her blood sugar, to do? Hello Chocolate Black Bean Muffins. I found a recipe, added my own twist to it and have been enjoying dessert ever since. It's made with cocoa powder, maple syrup and a dash of cinnamon (cinnamon naturally brings out the sweetness in recipes).

If you have a sweet tooth like me, go to www.HealthierBodyHealthierBusiness.com to download this recipe.

Here are some ingredients to use to naturally bring out the sweetness in foods and beverages without having to add sugar:

1. Cinnamon

2. Vanilla

3. Unsweetened Applesauce

4. Stevia

5. Coconut

I have tried THIS diet and THAT diet and started using products with way too many artificial ingredients. I thought I could eat all the "sugar free" and "diet food" I could find and that would be the end of that. It didn't work. I gained weight, and to this day, I can't stand the smell of steamed broccoli.

I slowly started to make a few small changes to the foods I was eating. I started eating more complex carbs and fibre and less refined sugar and "fake foods". It took a few weeks, but eventually, the weight started to come off. That's all it takes. If you lose at least 5-7% of your body weight, it has an AMAZING impact on your blood sugar.

WHAT IS PREDIABETES?

Before diabetes, comes the diagnosis of prediabetes. "Pre" meaning before. You know like, preschool…before you go to school. Preteen…before you become a teenager. Or, for some of us, prenup…before you lose all your money to Mr. or Mrs. Why-Did-I-Marry-You-In-The-First-Place?

Prediabetes usually occurs because you're a little overweight, not a lot—maybe only needing to lose 5-7% of your bodyweight—and because your blood sugar is too high. Typically, it manifests itself by causing you to not feel good; you don't have enough energy and it impacts your work, and therefore your income, profitability and ability to make money. You started a business to be successful; don't let prediabetes get in the way of what you can achieve for yourself and your family.

Prediabetes refers to blood sugar levels that are higher than normal, but not yet high enough to be diagnosed as Type 2 diabetes. There are no definitive symptoms of prediabetes. You can have it and not even know. If left unmanaged, prediabetes can develop into Type 2 diabetes—which comes with complications that may include heart, kidney, and vision problems.

It doesn't have to be this way. You can take steps to manage your blood sugar and change your future to one free of Type 2 diabetes. Ask yourself: what's the point of working as hard as I do? Building an incredible business should not come at the expense of your health. A healthy business needs a healthy business owner.

YOU MIGHT HAVE PREDIABETES & NOT EVEN KNOW IT

If you eat like most Canadians or Americans, chances are good that you have prediabetes and don't even know it.

Prediabetes is becoming more common and is impacting the health and life of more and more people every day. An alarming number of our population have prediabetes or are on a path leading them to it.

Symptoms of prediabetes may include:

- Increased thirst
- Frequent urination
- Excess hunger
- Fatigue
- Blurred vision

Quite simply: when you lose weight and lower your blood sugar, you will have more energy and mental focus. When you have more energy and mental focus, you will be more creative, productive and have the ability to generate more income.

Repeat after me: "When I do right by my body, my body does right by me."

Raise your hand if you're stressed.

Raise your hand if you're not getting enough sleep.

Raise your hand if you're skipping meals and eating too much sugar.

Have you been told that you need to lose weight?

Have you been told that your blood sugar is too high?

Are you running a business and neglecting your health?

You're smart and started a business for a reason. You're brilliant and you work hard. You know the nutrition basics: eat your fruits and vegetables and drink plenty of water. But do you know the nutrition basics for high performers and entrepreneurs? Eat to support your brain, to keep those brilliant ideas coming, and eat for energy and peak performance. Think about it. What does an elite athlete eat? Or better said, how does an elite athlete fuel their body? How do they eat to maximize their performance?

Think of yourself as an athlete. Your sport is your business, and you need to eat to maximize performance.

FEED YOUR BRAIN & YOUR BODY WILL FOLLOW

Prediabetes has an impact on your mood, energy, productivity and brain health. A study in *Diabetologia* shows that there is an association between high blood sugar and long-term cognitive decline. The study found that the cognitive decline associated with prediabetes and diabetes has significantly increased.

Here are my 10 tips to Crack the *Rich Code* when it comes to your health and improving your business performance.

1. Eat for your brain and your body will follow
2. Eat more greens
3. Remove refined carbohydrates
4. Cut out artificial sweeteners
5. Limit sugar
6. Increase fiber
7. Load up on antioxidants
8. Read nutrition labels
9. Eat more fat (the good kind) and eat less fat (the bad kind)
10. Eat more raw foods

We all know those people that skip breakfast, fill up on junk food and have never found a vegetable they liked. Maybe you're one of them.

Your brain needs fuel. Your brain needs iron, magnesium and essential fatty acids. Your body needs fuel. Your heart needs COQ10, your muscles need magnesium, and your eyes need lutein. A healthier you is a more productive you. A more productive you, makes more money and simply accomplishes more personally and professionally.

Food for people like you, isn't just for taste or pleasure. It's for function. It's fuel. Fuel your brain, mood, energy, creativity, stamina, productivity and concentration. Creativity and innovation live in a brain that is well fed and well nourished. Energy and a positive mood come from a body that is well rested, pampered and hydrated. When you eat better, you feel better, you look better and you have more energy to do whatever you want—more work, more family time or just more ME time.

What happens if you keep eating badly, continue to gain weight and your blood sugar continues to go up? You're headed for Type 2 diabetes and studies show heart disease too, which could mean a lifetime supply of insulin, other medical conditions, more medication and the loss of future profits and income.

Imagine waking up 5 years from now in the same condition or worse.

KNOW YOUR NUMBERS

You're probably familiar with your ROI, P&L and COG. Do you also know your A1C? Your A1C (also known as the hemoglobin A1C or HbA1c test) is a simple blood test that measures your average blood sugar levels over the past 3 months.

Prediabetes left uncontrolled becomes diabetes and can lead to negative consequences. Ladies, think candida fungus—which causes yeast infections and thrush. Gentlemen, think erectile dysfunction and low testosterone.

You're more likely to get prediabetes if you:

- Are overweight (especially if you have extra pounds around your belly)
- Have a waist larger than 40 inches (men) or 35 (women)
- Eat and drink sugary foods and beverages
- Avoid exercise
- Have a history of gestational diabetes
- Have a parent, sister, or brother with Type 2 diabetes

Race and ethnicity are also a factor. If your background is African, Hispanic/Latino, Indian or Pacific Islander, you are at higher risk.

HEALTHIER BODY, HEALTHIER BUSINESS

Think back to this morning. Breakfast. Did you have any? If so, was it filled with what your brain needs to fully be optimized? If you had coffee, how many teaspoons of sugar did you put in it?

Some of you are finally realizing your business goals and dreams. It's time to make sure you're healthy enough to truly enjoy it. In your business, if you need help with marketing, you hire a marketing director. If you need help with day-to-day tasks, you hire an assistant or virtual assistant. If you need help with your graphics, you hire a graphic designer. When it comes to your health, it's all up to you. Only you can make these changes. When it come to learning the steps necessary to improve your health, you can't outsource this; only you can make the changes, but you can ask for help.

When faced with a challenge at work or in your business, you make a decision and take action. Some of you are now faced with a health challenge. You need to decide and act! That's what I did. I made a decision, and I took action. I reduced the amount of sugar in my diet and made small changes that have benefitted me personally and professionally.

This pandemic has revealed how important our health is. If you noticed that your sales or labour costs were headed in the wrong direction, what would you do about it? Your blood sugar and weight are headed in the wrong direction. What are you going to do about it?

Be proactive.

This is not about fad diets, trendy foods and diets that completely cut out entire nutrients that can negatively impact your metabolism. You can't completely cut out entire groups of macronutrients. You need Vitamin B for energy and Vitamin K for your bones and skin.

You might be thinking, *"I don't have time for special diet food, overpriced diet food. Plus, I'm a bad cook."* Me too. Or maybe you're thinking, *"I can't afford fancy exotic food."* If you can read a recipe, own a blender, or can learn to make smart choices when dining out, you can do this.

Maybe:

- You've been recently diagnosed with prediabetes
- You have a family history of diabetes
- You're tired of holding your stomach in when taking photos
- You're tired of being tired all the time

My biggest challenge and frustration were trying to make sense of the information out there. Whole wheat or whole grain? Coconut sugar or Splenda? White potato, sweet potato, no potato? Weight training or cardio? I'm not about deprivation. All you need to do is make a couple of tweaks to what you're doing now. It's not a diet. It's a lifestyle change.

Imagine how much better you'll feel when you've lost weight and don't have to hold your tummy in anymore. Imagine having more energy to work longer and harder if you want. PLUS, you'll be able to fit in your pre-pandemic clothes again.

WHEN YOU KNOW BETTER, YOU DO BETTER

If you're not healthy, you can't put into your work or business what you need for yourself, your staff or your clients. You need optimal brain power and energy. You need to be creative, in a good mood and have the energy to get you through the day. You need to be able to execute, keep focused and stay on track.

So, for those who want results and want to get off the one-way train to diabetes, heart disease, and a host of other unpleasant conditions—those who are ready to take their health, and therefore their business, to the next level—let's connect.

Let's get your health back on track so you have the energy to run your business or work your way up that corporate ladder.

Go to www.healthierbodyhealthierbusiness.com to download the recipe for Chocolate Black Bean Muffins and take my 5-Day No Sugar Challenge.

For information about how we can work together, feel free to book a free consultation with me so we can get started.

***

To contact Andria:

Schedule your call with me at:www.MeetWithAndria.com

To Download the recipe & take the 5-Day No Sugar Challenge, visit my website:

www.HealthierBodyHealthierBusiness.com

To Learn more about Andria Barrett, visit my website:

www.AndriaBarrett.com

Yolanda Martinez

Yolanda Martinez is an evolutionary work in progress, just like you! Yolanda has a unique approach to feminine leadership and her impact is huge. Her story did not begin here. Yolanda was born in Apatzingán, Michoacán, Mexico. She grew up in Oregon and Washington, where she worked as a migrant worker with her family from 7 until she graduated from High School. Her father taught her the value of money and self-respect. Yolanda ventured off on her own to LA at the age of 20. Yolanda's adventures began in LA, where she was in the education industry for ten years and in the fashion industry for over 25 years. Yolanda is a certified Makeup Artist; she loves giving back by empowering and helping women get back in the workforce to help them be independent and positive role models worldwide. Today Yolanda is an exceptional role model she helps women find their inner power by teaching them the value of self-care, self-love, and self-worth. She is the creator of 21 Days with Yolanda, an online program that touches on those elements. She celebrates her clients every day, but beyond that, she celebrates their lives, self-determination, their love stories, and their womanhood. Yolanda can't be accurately described in a short biography; she is a mystery that pays to uncover. She makes you feel; she inspires you to soar; she helps you evolve and is right by your side.

My past is my motivation

By Yolanda Martinez

Have you ever been driving down the freeway and look over and see a massive farm with migrant workers in it? They may be picking strawberries, cucumbers, berries, or anything that seems to grow that needs a person to pick and harvest. What goes through your mind when you see the workers out in the hot field, bent over, working all day long? Do you say, "I sure wish I could do that?" "They are so lucky, what a great job, they must be making a lot of money," I seriously doubt that any of those thoughts go through your head. Most likely, you wouldn't take a job like that no matter what it paid.

Throughout my life, I have often heard women say, "You don't know me or my past." Let's understand something first: I get it...I know that everyone has a past, and some are not that great. Some are even so bad that you wonder how that person even survived. I have learned one thing in life, the pain we feel today and have from our past is because we have not gotten the lesson yet. Once we get the lesson, the pain goes away. This lesson will help us be aware that we will never give up our power to anyone or anything from the past. We let the pain empower us to create a very compelling future to inspire others. This chapter is about taking control of your life and knowing that you deserve to be happy and are here to make a difference in your life and many others. I will tell you that the only way that can happen is if you decide that you will no longer allow your mind or story from the past to hold you back and allow it to empower you. Are you up for this? Because if you are, then your life will be even better and on purpose. When we focus on what happened to us from the past, we are not serving anyone and will feel stuck and in pain. We have pain because we are focused on how we feel instead of helping others.

I'm not here to downplay some of the horrific events that have happened in your life; I am here to free you from your past so you can move forward and inspire, empower, and make a difference in your life and someone else's. I know about pain, and I also know about freedom. The next time you drive by and see a massive field with a group of migrant workers out there, maybe you can stop and take a moment just to watch them and see what you discover about them. Perhaps you will make conversation and find out what their story is before making any kind of judgments. Inquire about their pain and find out what they truly appreciate. You might be surprised to find out that what matters to them the most is having a job and feeding their families. Even though they are in a lot of pain, they realize that true wealth is their family and what they have, not what they don't have. From age seven until 18, I was that hard-working migrant worker in those fields, working from 5 AM until dark every day in the summer. While other kids were playing or going on family vacations, I was working; that was one of the greatest gifts my dad gave me. I learned from a young age that if I wanted something, I had to work hard for it and not depend on someone to get it for me. I learned that the same applies when working towards your goals and aspirations; YOU are the one that must work hard at accomplishing them because no one was going to come and do it for you. I had pain, I had pride, and I knew what I appreciated in life; for ten years of my life, I earned just enough money each summer to buy my school clothes and school supplies I was going to need for the year. Would you have done that and not complained as a child? Would you ever give your child/children this experience?

I only tell you this story, so you don't get the wrong idea that I was some prima donna that had things handed to her. This chapter will show you how you can take what you experienced in your past and maybe even now in your present life and make it even better. When I hear about people still in pain, I think back to when I was in the fields picking strawberries, and my back would start to hurt after a couple of hours of picking, and I realized that if I didn't do something different, that pain would only get worse. At a very young age, I learned that various strategies could be used in the fields and in life to ease the pain and make what I was doing more fun, more advantageous, and create value for each day. When I focused on the pain, it would worsen, my mood would change, and my thoughts turned to negative thoughts about what I was doing, and my earnings would be less for that day. All it took was one time to see the difference, how my way of thinking would give me a bigger reward at the end of the day, so I started focusing on how I could do things differently but still accomplish my goal. I often think of people like

Oprah, who have been sexually abused or molested in the past; what helped them take their pain and use it to motivate them to be successful and positive? Oprah created a movement and made sure that what she went through was never going to happen to her again, and she lived on purpose to help as many people as possible. Here she had everything taken from her, and once she created new meanings and stories, her life and millions of others were forever changed. Take your past and empower your future.

It's amazing how just making minor changes can affect your life in a big way. Imagine having these three steps to help you, so you thrive in this life and take control like you never have before. You get to create and decide what it is you want now and tomorrow. I have a 21-day experience that will get you the results you always wanted and didn't think you could have. I will get you on the path where you will feel and see results on the first day. Are you ready for this? I think you are.

1. What is your story?
2. What meaning does your story have in your life?
3. What is your purpose?

While my work ethic grew, so did my dreams. My self-confidence came from knowing what I wanted and planning how I was going to get there. When I was 14 years old, I asked my parents about modeling school; my father did not have to think about it, his automatic response was no, his idea of what modeling was did not fit in the plan he had for me. On the other hand, my mother told me she would take me to the school and sign whatever documents she needed to attend modeling school. In her eyes, I was doing something I wanted to do, and she knew that I would not stop asking, so she supported my dream of becoming a model. From that point on, I knew that I had to stand up for myself, fight for my dreams, and believe in myself when others didn't. I know that this powerful tool is what influences women today. Imagine if you had a program that could help you regain your power, encourage you to use your voice and own it, and give you the confidence to accomplish all of your dreams. In my "Love Yourself in 90 days–Unveiling the New You" coaching program, you begin with uncovering the limiting beliefs, blocks, and barriers that exist from your past that hold you back in the present. In doing so, we discover how self-love and confidence will help you create space to discover what you want and reveal the vibrant and confident person that is already there and waiting to come out. Clients tell me that with this discovery, not only do they genuinely know what they want, but it also helps them uncover who they truly are. They discover that self-love is critical in this journey. From this place of self-discovery, they now have the tools to self-navigate emotions and conflicts so that they no longer feel stuck, lost, or confused. What would your life look like if you could Maneuver through it with confidence and ease? What if you could learn to tap into your internal wisdom? What would you accomplish if you had the tools to help you get in the right mindset in seconds? Here's where the process begins for you; by going over your goals, visions, and intentions in the important areas of your life, you can see the life you want versus the life you have. What do your goals in Love & Relationships look like? How important is it to have a support system within your Family & Friends? Is being Healthy & Fit affect your emotional well-being, as well as Career & Finances? Discussing what you want to receive and let go of is part of this process that will get you to start living the life you have always wanted. When you put your story on paper, you can begin creating a personalized plan that will showcase your unique strengths and give you opportunities to move closer to your ideal life.

As I mentioned, I wanted to give you six tips that are about to change your life. Before I do that, I want to share a quick story with you that came at the perfect time, funny how things show up in our lives when we need them the most. It may sound familiar, but that's because it was just on America's Got Talent; often, my husband and I will sit down watch an episode or two. We like listening to everyone's "Life Story, see when you listen to someone's "life story," you can understand why they are where they are. When I talk to someone, I ask about their childhood, circle of friends, and what they want. While listening to everyone's story, we open ourselves to learning and having something positive and rewarding appear in our lives; just like that, it shows up. We thought a break from daily life would help us relax, and instead, it turned out to be a lesson in disguise, and I wanted to share it with you now.

We were just enjoying some quiet time watching America's Got Talent; a beautiful soul came out and stood in front of the microphone, getting ready to perform; something about her was radiant. Her smile was beautiful, but her soul showed pain. Howie asks her, "what is your name, and what do you do?" She says, "my name is Jane. When I sing, I go by Nightbird." "My dream is to be a singer; Howie then asked her, "what will you sing for us tonight?" She says, "it's an original song, called It's OK." Howie says, "It's OK, it's OK, what is It's OK, about?" She says, "It's OK is the story of the last year of my life." Howie says, "What do you do?" She says, "I have not worked for a few years; I have been battling cancer." Howie says, "I am sorry." She responds, "Howie, that's OK." Then Simon asks, "How are you now?" She responds with, "The last time I checked, I had some cancer in my lungs, my spine, and my liver." Howie then says, "So you are not OK?" She responds with a smile, "Not in every way, no." He says, "You got a beautiful smile and a beautiful glow that nobody would know." She says, "It's important that everyone knows that I am so much more than the bad things that happened to me." This statement impacted my core; how could someone who has a deadly disease be confident and optimistic? I realized where her glow came from, her mindset; she did not let the disease define who she was, and instead, it made her stronger to become the person she wanted to be.

Growing up I did not realize that my way of thinking was different from my family, my greatest guiding force was my strong mindset and because of that writing about this was hard. It has made me think and appreciate my past, even the tough times when the only person I could depend on and turn to was myself. It made me celebrate the fact that I honored myself first. I valued my myself and I did not let the things that happened in my life dictate who I become. I did not wait for things to happen for me, but instead I made things happen for me. As I mentioned earlier, your story will dictate how you move towards your goals. Your story will dictate the meaning you give it and how it will make you feel. And your mindset will be your guiding force in creating the life you want. I learned a long time ago that waiting for something to happen will always stop you from living life in the moment or to the fullest. As she began to sing her song, the relationship she was referring to was with herself, which is where all connections start. How can you ever love anyone or anything else if you don't love and appreciate who you are now? You don't let what you have been through in your past, nor what you are going through right now affect how you treat yourself? Whenever I coach clients, the most important thing I get across to them is their relationship with themselves. The power of self-care, self-love and self-worth will impact how people see you and how they will treat you. The entire song was about everything she was going through, and it was OK. As we are listening to her sing, my eyes tear up, and chills are going up and down my body and I am getting emotional; it was like an angel singing with a purpose to inspire everyone to stop and listen. When she finished singing, Simon was speechless, hard to believe but true, and just when you thought it couldn't get any better, she made a comment that will forever change how I see my life and how I coach clients. She said, "You can't wait until life isn't hard anymore before you decide to be happy." This phrase is significant to me because when I was around 16 years old, I started noticing that my dad always made promises by saying, "we will go do this or that soon, just wait until......" I always wondered, what was he waiting for? Why is waiting to do it later better than doing it today? I made a conscious decision that when someone said, "wait until" that did not apply to me because I always asked, "what am I waiting for?" See when someone says wait until, I always felt like that meant that they were still waiting for that something to happen to get them to move forward. For me waiting meant not living, not enjoying, and definitely not experiencing life to the fullest. My choice is to live my life to the fullest, waiting is not an option when my purpose is to inspire and teach. So, when she said this, my tears flowed, I realized how much I have to be grateful for, this amazing soul had a sense of peace within herself that inspired me, that is when Simon said, "I am not going to give you a yes," and as the audience got quiet, he stood up and said, "I am giving you this," he stood up and pushed the golden buzzer. This was indeed a golden buzzer moment; it wasn't her talent that was so impressive it was her confidence and her positive attitude that impressed the judges. That is what made this a compelling moment for everyone watching. It just shows you that you don't have to be famous to make a difference; but you do need to be your authentic SELF. We have nothing to prove, just something to share. When she got off the stage, she made a very powerful statement I have ever heard, "I have a 2% chance to survival, but 2% is not 0%, 2% is something and I wish people knew how amazing it is." and she smiled. Everyone has a right to live their life, but as I see some people alive, I also see those same people not living their life to the fullest, all because of the relationship and story they tell themselves because of a past event that happened to them.

You are about to change your story and you will focus on what you have and appreciate it to make a difference in your life and the relationship with yourself, so you can make a difference in other people's lives as well. In my 21 Day's with Yolanda online program, the first thing I talk about is the relationship with yourself, how you treat yourself and others, and how you allow others to treat you and influence you. In the first few days, I would like you to ask yourself, to show up owning who you are, realizing that the only person who can honor, love and empower you is YOU. Honor yourself by creating a journey to discover who you really are and who you need to become to live the life that you have always dreamed of. Understand and discover what is important and what can you do to live your life on purpose based on the vision you have of your life, not the vision that society has influenced you to believe you wanted. Isn't it time for you to be on the path that YOU choose? In the next 21 days lets create you, the new you and develop new habits to honor who you are; where you now know who you really are, so you own your power and your voice as a role model for all women that are around you. Develop new habits for self-love, self-care and self-worth that influences those around you to ask, what are you doing different that makes you hold your head high and confident?

Here are the 6 steps to get started now:
- (1) Gaining clarity that helps growth;
- (2) Identifying and examining self-imposed limitations;
- (3) Creating a daily practice with weekly assignments that build healthy habits;
- (4) Reprogramming habits, thoughts, and beliefs—the breakthrough shift;
- (5) Defining what is critical for you; and
- (6) Regular celebration—acknowledgment of wins!

Your 21 Days with Yolanda online program, creates and helps women incorporate these six steps with daily action steps that helps you and others establish a routine that becomes part of your life and their life too. Each action step in based on developing new habits that will motivate you to move closer to your ideal life!

***

To Connect with Yolanda:

Phone number 1 (702) 840-4968

Website: https://21dayswithyolanda.com

Facebook: https://www.facebook.com/yshoegal

Instagram: https://www.instagram.com/iamyolandamartinez/

LinkedIn: https://www.linkedin.com/in/yolanda-martinez-24606913/

Dawna Campbell

Known as the Mind Whisperer, Dawna combines her past knowledge, wisdom, and experience to assist you in creating and restoring a life of happiness, prosperity, and love. Dawna has over 25 years combined years of professional experience. As a former Financial Advisor, her book, Financially Fit, is a #1 Amazon International Best Seller bringing together the world of money and the energy body, and the souls essence. She is a professional speaker sharing her techniques during interactive workshops and maintains an international private practice. Dawna has shared the stage with Lisa Nichols, Dr. Joe Vitale, Sharon Lechter, and David Meltzer. Her personal *Heart Centered Healing* philosophy is to create a world that is a better place for all to live.

Infinite Prosperity Secrets

By Dawna Campbell

Everyone wants to live a prosperous life with happiness and love. These are the qualities that people seek from all around the globe. A favorite movie of mine full of wisdom is the Wizard of Oz. Glenda, the good witch, said to Dorothy, "You've always had the power, my dear; you just had to learn it yourself."

The power to gain infinite prosperity is always inside. Often, we feel stuck, unable to access this internal power, feeling like a failure in life. These feelings return beliefs about ourselves, such as being wrong, unloved, not enough, unworthy, undervalued, or unappreciated. Many of these feelings are created from childhood experiences and stop us later in life from stepping into our internal power.

What is stopping you from stepping into your power to gain infinite prosperity?

I allowed my mother, unknowingly, to stop me from stepping into my power to gain prosperity.

Saturday Mornings

Every Saturday morning after breakfast, the weekly chores were next. Dishes, vacuuming, and cleaning the bathroom were usually assigned to me. The prize for finishing the chores is escaping to the freedom of the great outdoors.

Except, this morning, my mother caught me at the back door. She asked me, "Dawna, what do you want to be when you grow up?" Excited, I knew I had the perfect answer and shared my heart's desire! I looked up at her innocently and replied, "Well, I am going to join Green Peace and save the whales!"

Lightning flashed through my mother's eyes, and with her penetrating death ray stare, "Dawna!" she said, "you can be anything you want in the world – be a doctor, a lawyer, or even a scientist!" Opening the back door, she stormed through, slamming it behind her, choosing not to speak to me the remainder of the day.

"What did I do wrong?" I wondered, quietly slipping out a different door. "What happened"? Rationalizing, I made a decision. I would tell my mother what she wanted to hear. Maybe being a teacher or a veterinarian would make her happy.

With the answers of telling my mother what she wanted to hear, a vast pain accumulated in my heart space — feeling less than, not enough, and unable to follow my heart's desire became unbearable, but necessary to avoid the fear of disappointing my mother.

Conditioning

The women's liberation movement was at the peak height in the 1970s while living in Silicon Valley. Social conditioning and pressure were experienced and placed on women. For the next generation, opportunities for women to work in a "man's" world opened up. The ability for women to produce a high income and be married raising a family became a reality.

Growing up near the poverty line, our family struggled financially. As the only girl in the family, my mother pushed me into this new lifestyle, believing that was the best for me. She wanted me to experience and have opportunities she didn't have. The conditioning ignited a passion within for helping families financially. I desired to help middle-class America provide opportunities for their families, repeating the same subconscious pattern taught by mother with providing opportunities for others.

My career path became financial planning, being responsible for $500 Million of other people's money. Excelling on the fast track, I became one of the first women to join the ranks of the upper management at a National Investment Firm.

Stress slowly set in and brought a series of emergency room trips without a conclusion over several years. I sought natural medicine and learned that food was not digesting, which stemmed from not emotionally digesting the stress, worry, and anger in life. My marriage quickly ended, followed by the global recession, leaving me devastated financially while following all the money rules.

Something was missing in this formula.

The Medicine Woman

While on a personal quest to uncover the missing pieces to living a prosperous life of happiness and love, I met a Medicine Woman.

The Medicine Woman was an older lady of around 70, with long grey hair always in a bun. She was a little plump with round-rimmed glasses and looked just like Mrs. Doubtfire, from the famous movie starring Robin Williams. The Medicine Woman was loving, nurturing, and kind, the very opposite personality of my mother, and not what I expected being the medicine woman on an Indian reservation.

The Medicine Woman taught this incredible strategy that opened up the doorway for uncovering three secrets to gain infinite prosperity. This strategy empowers you to live with infinite abundance and prosperity. Strangely, she was like Glenda, the good witch guiding Dorothy to step into her power.

Pivot and Shift

The Medicine Woman had me share my childhood story of growing up in poverty the way I remembered it. In great detail, my version sounded like a factual documentary. She had me repeat the story, but this time, I had to share the story of poverty from a place of comedy. The old Indian lady believed if there is a life review at the end of earth life, you might as well laugh walking on the blue road of spirit.

The next version came as a sad, tragic love story. I delivered the classic tale of Romeo and Juliet, where everyone died with a plot twist of the family fortune stolen by thieves.

After each version of the story, heaviness set in being tired from the storytelling. "Is there a point to this teaching?" I asked. All The Medicine Woman did was smile and ask for the next version to be delivered from the perspective of happiness, richness, and abundance. I returned the storyline with a huge smile! The most uplifting, heartfelt story of how I could help all of humanity through the spirit of generosity flowed out of me.

But I wasn't done. The Medicine Woman had one last version for me to share. She wanted to hear the same story of poverty from the viewpoint of a higher power that created me. The feelings and sensations felt inside were euphoric, magical, and love never felt before. Instantly I understood a greater truth.

The higher power that created me version became my new story.

The first teaching in using the pivot and shift strategy was complete—many more lessons with the strategy followed during the months after. The teachings continued until The Medicine Woman determined that I had the ability to use this gift and share it with the world to create instant change for others.

Everyone has the power to create reality by taking the original feeling and pivot and shift the feeling to live in a new truth. The new feeling generated is a new truth that to live. The best part is that it happens instantaneously once the undesirable feeling is recognized. Using the pivot and shift strategy is at the heart of my international practice with clients today.

The First Secret

"Hey, mom?" I innocently asked at Lucky's, a grocery store chain in California. "Can I have this slinky to play with?" finally summoning up the courage to ask. Slinky is a toy of coiled steel wires that arched, and when put in motion, it would take steps traveling. Fascinated, I saw it as a rainbow of joy walking.

"No," she said, without even looking. Probing, "why not?" realizing that it was only about $1, not very expensive in my mind.

Yelling, "Because we don't have the money. Dawna, Stop!"

In that instant, feelings of less than, not enough, and not worthy returned, flushing my cheeks bright red full of shame. The energy pierced through my heart as if committing the biggest sin. Quick to learn, I never asked for another thing from my mother after that, understanding that it is wrong to ask.

When utilizing the pivot and shift strategy, one of the steps is to determine how to feel that is better. When reflecting, I desired to feel loved, valued, and worthy from my mother, not less than. These are the feelings not taught when I was a child.

The doorway opened to the first secret of living an abundant and prosperous life.

Money is Emotional

How a person feels about themself on the deep subconscious level is how money responds in that person's life. The subconscious mind records every moment in our life, similar to a movie reel, from when we are born to the day we leave the earth. Every feeling experienced is recorded in the subconscious and assigned to the events, giving this an automatic response pattern to live.

The problem is the awareness of the feelings recorded to each event accounts for 10% of the conscious process. The remaining 90%, people are simply unaware of the feelings and emotions experienced in each moment. The universe, other people, and the environment transmit the feelings, similar to a radio tower, sending and receiving signals. The feeling signals are received and returned to the sender 100% of the time, allowing life experiences.

The secret is how you feel about yourself on that deep subconscious level is how money, and everything else in life, is returned to you. From early childhood, these mind-conditioning patterns get programmed and directly influence the money supply.

If a person didn't feel worthy, the net-worth wasn't very high.

If a person didn't feel enough, there wasn't enough money to reach the goals.

If a person didn't feel valued, the value in bank accounts depletes.

If a person didn't feel secure, investment in financial securities didn't exist.

If a person didn't feel appreciated, the money accounts didn't appreciate either.

Through conditioned programming, experiencing a continuous pattern of "less than" and other similar feelings creates a cycle of internal harm, the opposite of love. People grow up believing that they are wrong, abandoned, and lonely.

Discovering how you currently feel about money and recognizing the mind-conditioned patterns that are ready to release allows you to start stepping into your power to gain infinite prosperity.

Secret #2

My mind drifted off while lying down on the front lawn with the sun shining. Life is an adventure to be lived, cherished, and experienced. Staring up at the sky, wondering how far I could see looking up.

Watching a plane fly by, my imagination wandered to all the places people could travel. Perhaps the plane is flying to China, I mused, to visit the ancient temples and gardens. What would China smell like when they got off the plane? Do the Chinese eat with chopsticks all the time, or do they have forks? Is there a fire-breathing Chinese dragon for celebrating the New Year? Is it true that that digging a hole through the center of the earth, people would end up on the other side in China? Did fine china come from China? My eyes slowly closed, floating away with the clouds.

"Dawna," my mother called, waking me from my daydream. Getting up, I stumbled back into the house. "Yeah?" I asked. "What were you doing? I need you to help me with your brother."

Absent-minded, I mumbled, "exploring China."

A Return to Happiness

Being outside is my happy place, away from the stress and worry about money that came from my mother. There is an intense pressure around having money that it seemed impossible to have any. Once you had money, you never really did get to keep it anyway. Saving seemed futile since there were always bills to pay.

Every feeling that a person feels happens on the inside is secret #2. There is not a feeling or an emotion that is outside of the physical body. The feelings fuel the thought allowing direct experiences in everyday life. The emotional state is why two people can experience the same event and have two completely different experiences.

The experience that someone has is directly associated with the emotional state of the person experiencing and the subconscious tape that is playing automatically in the background.

When a person feels internally happy, happiness returns through the experience. When a person feels depressed, the whole world looks depressing to them.

When a person feels angry, everyone is angry.

When a person feels at peace, peacefulness is in every moment.

When a person feels prosperous, prosperity builds and accumulates.

The big mistake is believing money, which is outside of the physical body, is responsible for physical, emotional, and mental happiness. Social conditioning interprets money at the center of internal happiness, claiming more money and more happiness. Money is the carrot dangling in front of our eyes when the lack of money feeling magnifies.

Money is an external energy exchange source and responds directly in life according to how a person is choosing to feel. Stress, worry, and fear stop money flow while happiness, joy, and peace return money.

Identify what brings you true happiness on the inside. Using the pivot and shift strategy, when feelings of stress, worry, or fear are felt around money arise, take a moment, and breathe. With each breath in, recall what brings happiness. With each breath out, release the stress.

Returning to happiness will bring back your internal power and attract more abundance and prosperity into your life.

The Last Secret

"Today is the Day!" I exclaimed as my eyes lit up. While driving down the road, feeling much like a small child bouncing up and down on a sugar high. One of my greatest dreams is coming true. Today is the day I am moving to my new home.

I made a promise to myself that I would return to live in this place of beauty. My destiny is to live surrounded by nature, loving the outdoors. I desired a home with a feeling of living in a treehouse with lots of windows and a view of the warm sun greeting me, rising every morning over mountains.

Purchasing a home was not easy. After being financially devastated, it took many years of credit repair, unsure if owning a house was possible again. Mortgage lenders all agreed that having a home loan was impossible. The housing market was vastly different. Houses are double the price for a similar home where I currently lived. Renting a home wasn't an option being two times the mortgage payments.

A miracle happened. Keeping the faith, trust, and belief, the house loan was approved. Love poured out and spilled all over. Life instantly transformed, waking up every morning full of gratitude and acknowledging today is the luckiest day ever. "There is no place like home," as Dorothy would say.

Having a sacred space to live and maintain a balance of service to others is my motivation for purchasing a home. Alignment in heart, mind, and soul are essential qualities. When these three qualities are in unison, energy is abundant, limitless, and instant creation is possible, including with money. The ability to empower heart-centered business owners with this alignment allows you to step into your power and gain infinite prosperity.

Money Motivation

Money is becoming more significant and the external reward to receive money for being in the workforce, making investment choices, and offering services is a strong motivation. Social conditioning teaches money is the reward for an exchange of gifts and talents. Producing income is one way to avoid feeling the pain of the lack of not having. The problem is we are filling ourselves up with things from external sources rather than from internal motivation.

When a group of the top 100 global business entrepreneurs asked for the top advice they could share, every person gave an internal reason why they were motivated to share their passion, product, or idea. Money, financial gain, or accumulation was not on the list. Some of the top advice is:

Love what you do, and you have got to do it.

Emotionally invest in yourself.

Believe in yourself, and others will believe in you.

Be an inspiration.

Foster your dreams, and they will become a reality.

How you are motivated to use money is secret #3. Applying the pivot and shift strategy can quickly transform motivation from pain or lack into heart-centeredness. From this perspective, opportunities open up, and motivation comes from generosity and kindness. The motivation to "why" people choose to do something changes when the heart space is open to giving.

The soul knows the pathway to happiness is through the service of generosity. The expression of generosity comes through kindness, an internal motivating factor of love and the heart's desire to do good deeds. Kindness facilitates generosity. The results are discovering gifts from the pain experienced when we live in harmony.

Silver Lining Gifts

The subconscious intention of every event experienced is to bring our awareness with a gift that is ready to be received. The gifts discovered may vary by person. Even with the most traumatic events in a person's life, there are gifts. Opening our hearts to receive gifts is the only requirement needed.

Opening the heart space is precisely the pivot and shift strategy The Medicine Woman taught. When the pain is discovered and released, the feelings can transform the feelings into silver lining gifts. Rather than staying stuck in life, we harness the power to move forward and step into our power to live a prosperous life of happiness and love.

It is time to step into your power and gain the fullest potential of infinite prosperity.

***

To contact Dawna:

Dawna contact info

Website: https://dawnacampbell.com

Social media:

Facebook: https://www.facebook.com/dawnacampbell811

Twitter: https://twitter.com/healingheartinc

LinkedIn: https://www.linkedin.com/in/dawnacampbell/

Instagram: https://www.instagram.com/healingheartinc/

You Tube: https://www.youtube.com/dawnacampbell

Careyann Zivich

Careyann Zivich is a graduate of the Institute for Integrative Nutrition, an avid researcher and financial freedom coach. She lives in Ohio with her two sons and husband. After her first child was born, she was diagnosed with chronic fatigue syndrome and hypothyroidism. She overcame great difficulties with little support, which helped transform her into the powerhouse she is today. In September of 2019, she discovered a product with specific protocols used by medical professionals that she was able to utilize at home. That product became the foundation for her ascent out of chronic illness. She was determined to find a solution to not only all of her symptoms, but also to help others navigate their way out of theirs. The various wellness products she now advocates strongly for have become instrumental in her ability to help others find their way back to optimal health. Using the latest version of her foolproof system to promote one of the most beneficial supplements on the planet, she was able to generate six figures in under three months using organic Facebook marketing strategies. Since then, she has been helping others attain financial freedom and transform their own lives using the same system. If helping others both with their health and their income is something that you're passionate about, reach out to join her organization!

Help Others Grow and Unlock Abundance

By Careyann Zivich

Align Yourself with People Who Complement Your Weaknesses

Step into your purpose. It's found in your passion. The energy we give out to others is compounded and comes back to us tenfold. Always send out positivity. Helping others reach their goals and dreams helps you to reach yours. Collaborate. Two heads are better than one.

Where Focus Goes, Energy Flows

We all have disappointments in life. Before I learned how to transform my frustrations and anger into creativity and passion, I internalized everything, which made me horribly ill to the point of being unable to function from the weight of the negative emotions I was internalizing. The key to not allowing negativity to affect you is to channel your energy into something positive that can help you achieve the goals you've set. The first step lies in knowing what you want out of life and writing down your goals of where you would like to see yourself in the future. Anger and frustration can be used as powerful tools to achieving your goals when you learn how to harness and transmute that energy into something positive. Help others grow. It's rewarding, and in the process will help you grow along the way. Always look for the silver lining in the clouds. Sometimes the greatest pain can turn into the greatest blessing. The most difficult times in your life are what strengthen you to become what you were destined to be. The day you discover your "Why", the pain from your past will turn into gratitude. Your purpose can often be found in the midst of your deepest struggle.

Change Your Programming to Change Your Life

We all have pre-programmed responses to certain situations in life we carry with us from childhood adversity. The only way to change your life is to change the subconscious programming that is running 95% of your unconscious and automatic responses to everything that happens in your life. One of the tools that made the biggest impact in my life was hypnotherapy. You can reprogram your subconscious mind to make different choices when presented with situations you would typically react negatively to. If you want to change the people and things around you, change the way you REACT to them. When you learn how to RESPOND, instead of reacting from a place of pain or suppressed emotional energy from your past, the people around you also begin to make shifts. What you allow persists. It's up to you to set boundaries with others. When you learn how to respect yourself, you won't allow certain behaviors to persist, and you will be able to make it further ahead in life.

Aim High and Believe in Yourself

YOU are capable of success. What do the successful have in common? They set goals while directing their focus and energy into making them a reality. I rarely watch tv or waste time on things that don't contribute to my personal growth, the growth of others or my happiness. How much time do you spend on things that are not elevating you or moving you one step closer to achieving your goals? Fill your down time with actions that will propel you towards the life of your dreams. Duplicate what other successful people are doing. Our organization trains people on duplicating our proven system of how to become successful in the network marketing industry using social media marketing. Our resources are currently provided free of charge to anyone who enrolls under our team. You're worthy of financial freedom, abundance and vibrant health. Focus on your end goal, not on the obstacle. What thoughts continually run through your mind? Are they predominantly positive or negative?

Change Your Thoughts to Change Your Future

You CAN switch your focus to a better feeling thought even in the midst of adversity. You CAN elevate your vibration by simply choosing to focus your energy onto a more positive thought when you're down, even if you're surrounded by negative people. You get to choose what thoughts and memories dominate your mind each second. The more you focus your mind on positive thoughts and memories, the more abundance you will be able to attract into your life.

Gratitude Is the Gateway to Abundance and Bliss

Remind yourself to remain in a state of gratitude. What can you do to help improve someone else's life today? What can you do to make your dreams a reality? Write down your goals on a sticky note and read them every morning when you wake up. This will program your subconscious mind to finding ways to make them a reality. Level up with me and learn how to create a conscious income online by sharing some of the most amazing health and wellness products on the planet! If you're ready to completely elevate your ENTIRE life, go all in with what you choose to pursue. You need to be committed to self-expansion and remain open to possibilities and opportunities.

What would an extra $500 a month do for you?? How about an extra $500 a week or $500 a day? That's the potential income you could make and more by promoting superior products in the network marketing industry. Start a home-based business today! There are so many opportunities that allow you to join their organization and start your own business for anywhere between $1-1000!!!

Find Something You're Passionate About and Share it with Others

If you're ready to live a life of passion and purpose, get in touch with me and we can get you plugged into our system that teaches you how to help yourself while helping others. Learn about the product you're promoting and its value. Do you have a passion for learning? Do you thrive on living your dream life, your BEST LIFE? Are you a team player? You become like the 5 closest people you surround yourself with, you embody them, their actions and their thoughts. Find and surround yourself with people that inspire you to elevate yourself, find people that have forged the path ahead of you, find people that are ready to support YOU. If you love being involved in educating others and being a part of a thriving community, then I'd love to invite you jump in and contribute to not only your success, but also the success of others, by sharing your gifts so that we can all thrive together both in health and financial freedom. We have members in our training group from every walk of life, and they all have unique gifts to share.

Always Look for the Opportunity Within the Risk Vs The Risk in the Opportunity

You can choose to allow fear to run your life, or you can choose to move towards your dreams and goals by facing your fears. What fears are holding you back from moving forward in life and what steps can you take to overcome those fears?

Stop Selling and Seek to Provide Value

Your income is a reflection of the value you have brought to the world. Know your product. You can't market something well if you are not versed in how it works and what benefits it can offer your potential clients. No one is going to learn it for you - YOU need to understand how your product works and how it can solve your clients' problems. Unplug. Consolidate and eliminate actions that are not going to further your skills, knowledge, business, or future. Your time is valuable, and so are YOU – make it count. When you educate people with resources on why a particular product will be beneficial to them, while giving them the option to choose, they no longer meet you closed-off. Send them studies and resources. When people can read and see for themselves how beneficial your product is, it empowers them to make their own decisions.

I spend the majority of my time researching and providing resources. People will ask you where to purchase your products instead of you chasing them if you provide them with the tools, and the knowledge they need to help themselves. When you can switch people's focus from "my doctor said there is no way to reverse my symptoms" to "there might be a solution to my problem", it can create a powerful shift in their lives.

Join Us to Change Lives, in More Ways Than One

Join our organization to learn how simple it can be to live a life of financial abundance and freedom and how quickly you can get there using an easy, duplicatable system EVEN IF you can barely function. The network marketing industry can be a four-year career for some. With superior products, it's easy to make a difference, help yourself and others get back to optimal health while helping them also earn an income by sharing a product they not only love but one that helps improve people's overall quality of life!!! The best part?

It can take as little as a single dollar to get started!!! Even the homeless could start earning money to get themselves out of poverty by using our system!!!

> "If you don't find a way to make money while you sleep, you will work until you die." ~Warren Buffet

> "You're never too young to launch your empire, and you're never too old to inspire someone to build theirs."~Richard Bliss Brooke

The secret to success lies both in duplication and collaboration. I learned a system that worked from someone I admired and improved upon it. Trying to sell people products by being pushy or desperate does not work. Offer people value. Help people. The energy you put out comes back around to you. It's how the universe works. When you come from a place of wanting to make a difference, instead of from a place of "I need to make a sale" which emits lack, that comes across in your conversation. The first thing you should be asking people is "what symptoms are you attempting to improve?" Based on their answer, you can provide them with resources they can use to educate themselves on why they need this product.

Be a Problem Solver

Learn about the many benefits of your product. If they decide to buy your product or not should be left up to them. You're simply there to educate them and give them the tools they need to improve their lives and health. If you offer them value, they will come back to you and ask you where to buy the product without you ever having to push them into anything. Offering value builds trust. I've been a health coach for a few years now - I've charged only two people for actual hour-long sessions because they asked to pay me. Everyone else, I've helped for free. I've made more money helping people for free than I'd ever make spending hour-long sessions with them thanks to network marketing. The key is to get behind a superior product that gives noticeable results both quickly and effectively. If every health and wellness product was set up with the network marketing model, doctors would not have to charge people for treating them because the compensation plan would offer enough of a reward.

Instead of coaching people personally, I give them the tools they need to educate themselves. On what level you can replicate what I do depends on the time you have to devote to learning all you can about the product you're promoting and the time you spend going through the resources we have provided. I can confidently say that in all my years of trying hundreds of health products that took too long to work, and spending thousands of dollars in therapies and pills that didn't eliminate the root cause, the two main products I use now with all my clients could be the missing link you're looking for that can help to improve a plethora of symptoms. Due to the many symptoms, I've been able to reverse in my own life, I'm very passionate about helping others restore their health, because I know what it's like to wake up every day wishing for the day to end, only to repeat it all over again the next day and year. Whatever you're attempting to share with others, you should be fully educated on. If you're unsure of the benefits and value of your product, you will not come across the same way when sharing it with others.

Why I Advocate for Network Marketing Products Superior MLM products gave me my health and life back. In the process of giving me my health back, they also helped me earn an income to support my family and pay our bills when my husband fell off a roof and was unable to work. Superior MLM products gave me the ability to send my children to a Montessori school. Superior MLM products have allowed me the opportunity to help hundreds of other people in the same situation I was in to improve their quality of life and attain financial freedom when they couldn't find the strength to get out of bed. In their process of healing, they've been able to help countless others. My goal in life is to create a cascade of people who are helping empower as many other people as possible. I offer all of my resources and education for free to my organization so that we can all help others rebuild their lives and regain their health. Why? Because when I was ill, I had no one to help me and I had to find solutions on my own when I was barely functional. I spent every waking second researching and watching documentaries put together by the top functional medicine doctors in the industry, even though a majority of it I couldn't retain. Just because a company chooses to spend its money paying their sales force (moms and dads and regular joes) to promote a product so that they can spend more money improving the quality of their products and rewarding their sales force instead of dumping money into advertising or stocking store shelves, doesn't mean it's a scam. The network marketing model is just a model, a choice of how to set up a business. I want to change the face of network marketing. I want the stigma to go away. I want people to work together for the common good and to help each other. I want people to be educated and make their own decisions. **Educate. Inspire. Help.** Stop selling. Start caring. Start helping. No one wants to get spammed about your product. If it's a good enough product it will sell itself without you ever having to push your product or opportunity on your family and friends. Make it a priority to help others. Make it your goal to change the world with your unique gifts. That's one of the keys to success. Follow your passion and put your heart and soul into whatever you're doing. I'd rather support a mom and dad than support companies who pay their staff upwards of $7/hr. With MLM companies, the sky is the limit - there is no ceiling. You can make as much money or as little money as your efforts, time and energy allow. You get to decide when to work and when to play. The most important aspect of joining any MLM is to thoroughly research the company and products you're promoting before jumping on board. Secondly you have to get along with the person or team you decide to align yourself with and they have to be able to support you by proving ample resources, so you don't have to work so hard by yourself to get your business of the ground. This will determine your level of success or failure to a large degree. If you sign up for a company with mediocre products and mediocre resources, you won't get very far at helping yourself or others. Align yourself with someone who complements your weaknesses and you'll become a force to be reckoned with. Chose companies with a track record of consistent growth and consistently raving reviews from its customers and brand partners. An amazing and superior product speaks for itself and WILL sell itself with minimal effort on your part. If you're struggling with your health or would like to join our organization, reach out.

***

To contact Careyann:

Email: quantumharmonicsllc@gmail.com

Facebook: Facebook.com/careyannz

Frida Bruhn

Frida Bruhn is a Life & Success Coach. She has been working as an actress, editor and speaker for more than 25 years. Frida lived years of her life on autopilot in constant flight and fight mode. By failing, doubting, trying, and getting up again and again, she finally broke the vicious cycle of perfectionism, hurt and repetition and left two toxic relationships behind. The one with herself and the one with others. Frida now lives an abundant life, committing to Freedom daily. As a trusted advisor, Frida coaches clients around the globe on overcoming perfectionism, finding purpose, success and fulfilment. In addition, she is a Corporate Development Team Ambassador for the Association for Coaching in the regions Germany, Austria and Switzerland. Within the AC she promotes the spread of high-quality coaching for individuals and businesses as an opportunity to face current and future societal challenges. Frida is inspired, coached and mentored by Jay Shetty, Rich Litvin, Steve Chandler and Jim Britt. As a proud mom of six powerful kids, she enjoys exploring the world with them.

Urgent Delete: Perfection

By Frida Bruhn

You might think hard-working perfectionists have an excellent chance to become very successful. Maybe you think it might be an attractive trait to consistently improve and spot any mistake if you want to become rich one day. Well, let me tell you, it is not. How do I know for sure? It simply was the one obstacle that stopped me the most from having success for many years. Over decades I have observed many others who struggle with the same issue. On your journey towards wealth, Perfectionism is a roadblock. Today I am a trusted advisor helping people overcome their Perfectionism and healthily achieve their goals. Informing individuals how to develop unconditional love and self-compassion is part of my approach. It is crucial to let go of deep, underlying fears. If you commit to your success and focus on your goals, the path unfolds to get where your Mind directs you. Then it only requires your consistency, your commitment to walking the walk and, by doing so, becoming unstoppable.

As a kid, I misunderstood what was required to become a go-getter. I thought Perfectionism was a great mindset to pursue any dream and would lead to success. I was confident that if you only dedicated your life towards what you wanted, you would get it, but you must become perfect at it first. So, I tried just that. Unfortunately, I was highly (today, I would say unhealthy) self-critical and constantly pushed forward in an attempt to outdo myself every single day. I was impatient and no fan of taking one step at a time. Instead, I felt the urge to jump through the tasks at hand.

On top of that, I thought that being kind to yourself after failing meant being dishonest. My mum was very harsh on herself, and I thought she was right to do so. "Kindness towards yourself" felt like lying to her. Therefore, honesty meant, also for me, beating myself up when I failed. As I wanted to become successful with what I was doing, my attitude led me to blame, shame, sadness and self-doubt.

I grew up on the northern Baltic coast of Germany, where my parents owned a small family hotel. I had problems at school. My teacher criticized my handwriting. I got detentions for it, alongside some children with severe learning difficulties, cognitive-behavioural issues, or extreme aggression. Sitting in the same room, I felt terrible. I asked myself what was wrong with me. I did not feel like I fit in, and at the same time, I thought that there must be a reason for me having to attend, too. It never occurred to me to improve the quality of my handwriting. It never got better. Instead, I contemplated everything wrong with me that qualified me to sit in the same room with all the tough guys. My mom worried a lot about my response and considered that I was an autist. My therapist said I was traumatized due to toxic family dynamics. Trauma is one cause of Perfectionism. I hated school and did not understand the way we needed to "learn "there. I was bored to death. Constant daydreaming and shutting off every time I felt like I was going to fail meant switching schools many times and taking 15 years instead of 13. I never was a fan of competitions because failure was always a possibility. Mediocrity was not my style. My grades were either very good or a catastrophe. I was always obsessed with learning new things, though. Long before graduating, I had already decided to become an actress to live as many lives as possible. To me, this seemed to be the best approach for living a perfect life. At the time, I thought this meant: Gaining profound life experience through many adventures. Learning new things all the time. Being famous. Having money and buying a beach house in Santa Monica. I had never been there, but it sounded like an excellent plan to me. I still think this beach house is a great idea, to be honest.

Perfectionism does not agree with human beings, and it certainly does not lead to becoming successful. It not only has the power to destroy careers but also relationships. Firstly, it attacks the relationship with yourself as you tend to criticize yourself more with spikes rather than love from the heart. As energy tends to reinforce itself, the negativity also corrodes your relationships with others. Furthermore, it leads to failure, health issues and the wrong choices. Perfectionism also teaches you how to stand in your own way regularly.

If you are a bit like me, you know how it feels. One day, I felt like I had life figured out. Then, the next day, I felt clueless about everything. I kept feeling the urge to do something extraordinary.

Unfortunately, that also meant that whatever idea I came up with sounded mundane after I thought it through. I ended up coming up with new ideas and tasks repeatedly until they seemed too tedious and dull to continue. Do you recognize this pattern? Over the years, I have worked as a sausage and fish seller, a movie extra, living doll Penguin mascot (who went around and spread flyers), bartender, topic researcher, direct seller for bureau gardening, shaman, editor, model, actress, speaker and radio DJ. I studied at two universities and switched courses at least ten times. Others admired me for only doing what I wanted to do, but in reality, this was only half of the Truth. Self-sabotage stopped me from doing just that in countless ways and situations.

When I started as a radio DJ, I was self-critical and dedicated to constantly improving. Slowly, I realized that this was not the norm. I worked day and night and did not sleep when nobody else seemed to try as hard. Instead of rethinking my patterns, I thought others would benefit from being more self-critical too. Rather than adapting and accepting that work was good enough, I got frustrated about mediocrity. I remember a situation in my early twenties when I drove my former husband crazy because I complained, cursing, and getting more frustrated when making dinner for Christmas. I put so much effort into this. You might have assumed Queen Mum and a bunch of Royals were coming over - but it was only the two of us and our newborn daughter. If not in the world, at least I wanted to have everything perfect at home. Even when I had achieved some of my goals, there was no way I could seem to enjoy temporary success. I was constantly looking for new challenges I could set for myself and ways to prove myself. And why is that? I thought my value was dependent on my achievements. I did not understand that if I did not learn to appreciate myself, I would always find ways to prove that I was not good enough. The deepest love one should have is the one for themselves, but I could barely stand me. Even external validation could not fill the void in me, but the lack made my self-saboteurs even more potent, and the urge to become perfect grew.

Hmm, does this sound like a successful strategy to you? There is a quote by Suzy Kassem: "Doubt kills more dreams than failure ever will." I would say the same about Perfectionism. You are probably beginning to understand why Perfectionists tend to achieve less and stress more than regular high achievers.

Perfectionism ≠ High Achievers

Having perfectionistic traits makes it very difficult to become excellent or achieve your personal best. Getting something almost perfectly straight can feel like you, as a person, are a terrible failure because you are never where you need to be. Things are never perfect.

Perfectionists and high achievers are similar in setting lofty goals and working hard to hit them. High achievers are, however, likely to experience satisfaction and excellence on the way. In contrast, Perfectionists keep at the same task even when failure is inevitable. They want to avoid feeling the pain, hurt, guilt and shame, but attract it instead by being tenaciously hard on themselves in less than successful situations. The good thing is, they often do not shy away from starting over again and again on various projects even after evident failure. They persevere as long as they can. Perfectionists focus continuously on the next thing that is not good enough, what needs to be improved and constantly drive through their Scarcity Mindset by anxiously spotting mistakes. High achievers can see positive results and focus on helping others to become better as well. Perfectionists are highly self-judgmental and demanding of themselves, so they are more likely to suffer from mental and physical health issues and are even more likely to die earlier because of the stress and pressure of punishing themselves. High achievers experience goals as their pulling force. Perfectionists are driven by fear to hit their goals. If they are not capable of doing it perfectly, they feel like they have failed. High achievers like to push their goals and are proud when they overdeliver, thereby outdoing what they thought they could. Perfectionists tend to set their initial goals out of reach like I did when I was determined to earn $450,000 in my first year as an entrepreneur.

While high achievers tend to be happier and more successful, perfectionists blame themselves if they do not reach their mostly unrealistic goals. High achievers enjoy the journey as much as the achievements. Perfectionists only have their eyes on the prize. Therefore, they experience less joy about growing and thriving. Of course, all the negative thoughts about their disappointments come at a price: They impact their mental and often physical health. Their fear of not getting a perfect result can make it very difficult for perfectionists even to start. They tend to procrastinate until they have immense time pressure. As a result, they cannot deliver the best results they could have had they started earlier. Worse, they skip doing the task altogether. One of my favourite writers, David Foster Wallace, once said that "If your fidelity to Perfectionism is very high, you will never do anything." The painful experience of constantly focusing on an unsatisfactory performance leads to a defensive attitude towards criticism and low self-esteem.

Perfectionism often is a trauma response and can be so compelling that this underlying root cause will show up in your life precisely in the moments when you seem to have it all. The biggest successes bring the biggest fear. Especially when you have achieved your goals, fear might show its face in ways that you could not have imagined. So, when perfectionists get to where they think luck is waiting for them, they will not find fulfilment but rather anxiety.

Studies have shown that perfectionists experience stronger negative emotions like anger, shame, anxiety and guilt. So, if you tend to beat yourself up for not getting the perfect outcome, you were aiming for and feel less worthy because of it, that sounds like Perfectionism.

When you cannot win, do you tend to give up easily? On the contrary, it may be a sign you have developed outstanding skills in avoidant strategies.

If you spot Perfectionism in yourself, you are not alone.

"As many as two in five kids and adolescents are perfectionists," says researcher Katie Rasmussen, who explores child development and Perfectionism: "We're starting to talk about how it's heading toward an epidemic and public health issue."

The writer and novelist Anne Lamott said, "perfectionism is the voice of the oppressor, the enemy of the people, it will strangle you, it will drive you crazy all your life, and it is the main obstacle between you and your fucking first draft."

The striving for excellence is not the issue. The harsh inner critic is.

"Perfectionists are pretty much awash with stress. So even when it's not stressful, they'll typically find a way to make it stressful," says Gordon Flett, who has studied Perfectionism for more than 30 years.

Narcissism and Perfectionism

It took me years to understand which old childhood behavioural patterns were still dictating my actions and decisions today. My main trigger became an emotionally abusive relationship and my absolute inability to leave. At this point, I already was a mom of six beautiful superheroes, wanting to be part of a perfect couple and an ideal wife. I could not let my dream of a loving family go because of my Perfectionism which showed up in the trauma bond. I could not accept that the relationship had no potential to work out. From a distance, it might have seemed perfect: We attended events together, had five mutual kids, and lived in a vast Villa. I could buy everything we needed. The Truth is, I was living in denial of the fact that I was emotionally manipulated by my partner, who took advantage of my desire to improve and beat myself up if anything went wrong continuously. On the surface, during the relationship, I was blaming him for treating me poorly. Underneath, a straightforward Truth determined all my actions: If only I were to be perfect, he would not betray me. It led me to feel more and more imperfect - until I experienced the whole variety of desperation, sadness, anger, breakdowns and drinking too much alcohol to numb my pain.

I sought out the help of terrific friends, several therapists and coaches, and it took all of my courage to leave finally. According to my core values, my kids were my anchor to do the right thing. My inner child was the one who kept me sane, with her humour and creativity, rebelling against Perfection. Soon the saboteur inside me continued the internal battle by pulling me into the hyper-focus mindset of creative work. Surprisingly, it was seldom "good enough "and sometimes "almost perfect," in my opinion.

During this time of my life, I got obsessed with reading everything about optimal (and not so optimal) personal development. For me, it was clear I needed to work on myself now from the very core. So, I started kickboxing and practising mindfulness to reconnect to my core strengths and values. Slowly I began to see results. While improving myself, I found my calling in helping ambitious and already high performing individuals enhance their lifestyle, professional and personal outcome. Now I work with visionaries and leaders to overcome Perfectionism, gain excellence, success, and create a fulfilled life.

How did I finally recover from Perfectionism?

Please do not ask how many first drafts I killed inside my head until I came up with this chapter. Overcoming Perfectionism is a lifelong journey. I am getting better and better at it, and the fun in life grows. I agreed to co-write this book with Jim Britt and Kevin Harrington because for 32 years, "writing my first book" has been the most reliable challenge to appear in my yearly list of New Year's resolutions. Guess what has been stopping me every single year? Correct: Perfectionism. So, I convinced myself that it does not need to be a book. Doing is the key. -- Getting the first draft on paper and taking action. A chapter is enough to get started. I knew these guys would hold me accountable.

How can you prevent, spot and overcome Perfectionism?

If you have children, my first suggestion is to create an environment of unconditional love for them. In an intimate family without children, it is equally essential to provide the same support and unconditional love to your spouse or partner. If you are single, create this just for yourself. Celebrate every day "being imperfect".

Let me repeat this. We need to not only accept imperfection but celebrate it! It shows we are human. Sara Blakely grew up with her dad asking at the dinner table: "What had she failed at?" If Sara said she had tried something, but it did not work out properly, her father would give her a high five. Thirty years later, in 2012, Sara Blakely became the youngest self-made female billionaire. She says: "Instead of failure being the outcome, failure became not trying. And it forced me at a young age to want to push myself so much further out of my comfort zone. "

You can try and feel what it is like to say: "No" to commitments that you already know will end with being overwhelmed. Letting go of the habit of always taking on too much and exhausting yourself might be helpful for you. Instead of ruminating on problems and imperfections without coming to a solution, try to disrupt the cycle of negative thoughts. Practice telling kinder messages to yourself.

Thich Nhat Hanh "Compassion is a Verb"

Try practising compassion. Replace your inner critic with a loving voice of guidance to calm down your internal enemy. It will not only help to hear less from your critic, but you might also overreact less towards other peoples' mistakes.

By reminding yourself of the pathway you took towards your accomplishments, you will realize your journey so far and how much you have improved overall. Think about the successes and how much you have learned from your experiences.

At JSCS school my supervisor Mira Butler said: "There is no such thing as failure. Only feedback." Remind yourself of all the things, savor these feelings about what you have accomplished in the past. Then, reflect on where Perfectionism has had a positive impact and where it has not.

When you spot tension, stress, overwhelm - recognize it. Take a break. Go out into nature, if possible, to a nearby park. You can do a simple, practical task that does not take much effort to consider, such as doing the laundry. Calming the Mind through Meditation and Mindfulness and training your awareness muscles are helpful methods to canalize and redirect your thoughts and feelings. Also, opening the window and taking some deep breaths can help to disrupt any patterns of thinking. If it is a fulfilling life you are striving towards, you cannot start too early on letting go of false Perfectionism. It might feel challenging but focusing on single steps rather than the end goal and staying as relaxed as possible always will get you there. The key is taking action. Go with 70% instead of never going with 100%.

The most important thing is: Everybody can have it all. We can all become what we are supposed to be and know we are, deep down within. We need to let go of the fear of not being good enough or even perfect. So, when you think about how you can crack the rich code for yourself, find out which underlying saboteur is stopping you. Is it a perfectionist or what else? As soon as you identify an enemy within yourself, acknowledge him kindly. Then make sure you are dealing with him accordingly. I am not kidding. You need to be very consequential in not allowing him to dictate your life. Be compassionate to him and send him kindly far, far away. And do not forget to wish him lots of fun ahead.

***

To contact Frida:

www.fridabruhn.com

www.aimbrighter.com

Judy Copenbarger

Judy Copenbarger, JD, CFP® AIF® is the profoundly caring, professional money guide who counsels individuals of all ages and families of all types on the facts and agendas of money.   A best-selling author, Ms. Copenbarger has penned several books, serving as a wise thought leader and financial fiduciary savvy about all family business and money matters.

With her technical background in law, strategic financial planning, taxation and investment management, Ms. Copenbarger puts it all in writing, to finally bring MONEY TRUTH to your life and into the lives of your entire family, forever.

As a sought-after international speaker for over thirty years and professional planner to families of substantial wealth, Judy understands what it takes to grow and sustain wealth and pass along a meaningful legacy to the next generations.

Ms. Copenbarger shares the process of *creating a legacy* in these pages, in her books, on social media and within her online financial mastery program. Each of her works considers every aspect of finance: Legal and Legacy, Taxation, Cash Flows and Cash Reserves, Insurances, Banking, Real Estate, Business Interests and Investments. Her work helps individuals apply MONEY TRUTH's wisdom and create their *layers of legacy.*

Her personal *layers of legacy* include decades of successful practices serving thousands of financially optimized families and businesses, an agricultural heritage, her organic vegetable and rare fruit farms, a history overcoming challenges, strong faith, and well-loved chickens.

Judy resides in Southern California with her husband of 36 years, Larry, who is also an estate planning attorney. Their five world-changing children also live in California.

How to be Rich Forever

By Judy Copenbarger

That's the money question, isn't it? We want to know exactly how to keep our wealth, once we finally master the acquisition of it. How can I grow and increase the money after I get some, and most importantly, how can I remain rich... forever?

Valid question. The answer is Legacy.

1. Choose Your Outcome

There is basic technology to creating a sustainable legacy. A simple five-step plan of action is manageable enough. The tricky part of the planning process for most people tends to be the specificity of the goals. Once you obtain clarity about the result you desire, the planning elements fall into place. You must consider the desired outcome in order to affirm that you are on the right track. Here are your proven five legacy steps.

1. Choose Your Outcome
2. Manage Your Money
3. Consider Your "Life Print"
4. Challenge Yourself
5. Take Specific Action

Once you choose the outcome you want, you are ready to move on to the management of resources. This may be as exciting as giving away a million dollars to charity or purchasing a home for each child. It may be a simple as letters written to grandchildren detailing your hopes and dreams for their life journey and character.

2. Manage Your Money

I have had the honor of serving families and small business owners over the past several decades by helping them fund legacies for their families, business successors and causes that they care about. Through specific estate planning, asset management and insurance strategic planning, each client is able to optimize growth of their resources, multiply their money for the next generations, and preserve generational wealth through appropriate taxation planning.

Although it is true that managing the cash and real estate portion of a legacy is important and is a valuable way to fund and sustain a legacy, it is not always the biggest factor in a successful legacy.

3. Consider your "Life Print"

On the shore of a beautiful beach in Hawaii, a story unfolds just beneath the surface of the sparkling blue water. A few meters from the beach, attached to the sandy ocean floor, you can see the cornerstones of a building that once graced the beach. Although the vitality and activity of the building is long washed away, the concrete and iron foundation of the building remains. This is the evidence of the structure which once majestically stood in this place, filled with life. This is what remains. It is the footprint of the building.

Each of us has a similar opportunity to tell our story. Although we don't physically leave a footprint or foundation upon our passing, we do, indeed, leave a "life print." Our Life Print is the impression that others have of us once we're gone. I encourage you to consider what your Life Print will be.

What would you like your Life Print to be?

People will often describe a legacy that they would like to leave. Your Legacy is not something you leave. It is something that you create.

This is worth repeating:

Your Legacy is not something you leave. It is something that you create.

So, what are you creating for yourself? What will they say about you when you're gone?

4. Challenge Yourself

Your legacy begins with a solid foundation. If you can help the next generation, use your ceiling as their floor, you would, wouldn't you? If people and causes you care about can begin their journey by standing on your shoulders and continue building what you've put in place, wouldn't you choose that for them?

In addition to empowering your children and their children by eliminating taxation, providing real estate cash flows, and sustainable income flows, there are important considerations for your legacy. Beyond the financial foundation, you can provide a sustainable legacy built from your character, values, experiences and life lessons. These are the legacy elements which truly represent who you are. This is your actual "Life Print."

Here's your challenge:

Consider what elements you want to include in your "Life Print" Legacy.

Mistakes

If you have ever made a wrong turn, left a professional position too soon, or missed a flight, perhaps you made a mistake. A seemingly mistaken path often morphs into something serendipitous in hindsight. Because you made the wrong turn, you avoided a terrible traffic jam. Shortly after you left a job, circumstances changed for the worse in the company. The flight you missed allowed you to make the personal connection with a relationship that has become invaluable. We are grateful when serendipity appears. These are the stories worth sharing. These are the stories that have profound impact upon our children, grandchildren and next generations. When others can learn from a mistake that we made, we share with them a gift of experience, and a gift of perspective.

Business

For many families, their business is a great portion of their legacy. Perhaps they inherited a business from a father or mother, who raised them in the business. Their children were subsequently sent off to school to master the art of running a business and returned to take the business to the next level. So how do you handle an unequal "fair" distribution of a business which may not have each child equally involved in the growth and passion of the business? How do you maintain equity and fairness when not all children are equally vested in the future of the business? How are the key players of the business to be treated? How could we protect the backs upon which the family business was built? How do we take care of those loyal workers? Creating a legacy by design is one way you can protect the interest of those who toiled alongside as the business began to grow and thrive. To learn more about designing your specific business legacy, attend a free course at www.JudyCopenbarger.com/truth.

Charitable Endeavors

Your legacy may include a desire to improve your local community and make a difference out in the world. You may choose to include the funding or continuing of humanitarian projects that you've enjoyed during your lifetime. If you have ever helped outfit a child's soccer or little league team with uniforms and equipment, you've experienced the joy of giving back. Perhaps you will want your work of providing musical instruments to the local music program to continue through others.

Values

You have an opportunity to express the values of your Life Print through the legacy that you create – while you are here. If you value education, you may consider setting up an educational foundation, or by providing funding for the education of your children or grandchildren through a 529 account educational funding program. You could also create a trust with the purpose of funding private, public or specialized education, using specifically designed legal instruments. If you value travel, perhaps a travel trust could fund the future of travel adventures, humanitarian mission trips, and cultural exchanges.

As a dear friend of mine was growing up, he shared a value with his father. The value was baseball. They both loved everything about it. They set a goal to visit every Major League baseball stadium through the years. They created many lifetime memories throughout the country, visiting the stadiums, attending the games, and documenting their adventures together. Although the goal had not been completed by the time his father passed away, the values, love and experiences have become part of their family's legacy.

My baseball-loving friend is now the father of twin boys, and they are continuing the journey. Every so often, the trio packs up to visit yet another City and a explore a new stadium. The tradition and value of baseball is alive and well in their family legacy.

Behaviors

Perhaps you have a habit of helping to comfort the homeless. The common practices that you have during your lifetime doesn't have to be a blessing in a vacuum. Others can learn from your stories of helping others. If you have been the family member that makes sure the holiday gatherings and celebrations happen, then it may be worth passing along the stories to the next generations. If you are the neighbor that assures that everyone living near you has support when it is needed, or you are the friend that organizes the cul-de-sac picnics and holiday parties, you may be surprised how these simple gestures could inspire others through your legacy.

Attitudes

Your attitudes are worthy of repeating and sharing through your legacy. In particular, your attitude about money can be invaluable for your children and grandchildren for many years. Perhaps you have developed an attitude about wealth that provides that it is desirable to obtain and sustain wealth. It is not money that makes people good or bad. Money is merely a tool. It is how people use this powerful tool that creates a reflection of attitudes and values. It's not necessarily a problem to pass some money along to the next generations.

There is an art to imparting wealth upon others without harming them. We are all aware of stories of people who received too much, too soon, and the result was harm to themselves or others. They weren't ready to handle the resources. They had less training, support or knowledge than they needed to manage. Perhaps someone took advantage of their lack of understanding about money. If you intend to leave a substantial sum to loved ones or causes you care about, consider the readiness of the recipients to handle what they will be receiving.

Here's a simple attitude about wealth that has helped my clients and family over the years. You may consider adopting this basic balancing technique. When it comes to money, 1. Use some, 2. Give some, and 3. Save some. Learn more about specific financial strategies in Judy Copenbarger's best-selling book, Money Truth & Life.

Family Heritage

In addition to where you are going, your life story includes the history of where you've been. Where you came from is part of the legacy you can create for those following in your footsteps. If you are blessed to enjoy a rich heritage of culture from other countries, celebrate! You can pass along the family traditions, favorite foods and cherished holiday recipes, and photos and videos of your ancestors. Share the stories of your parents, their parents. Help your children and grandchildren understand the triumphs and trials, the celebrations and struggles of your parents and perhaps your own. You can give this gift of understanding to the next generations that will not only raise their awareness of their heritage but gain a valuable perspective which could only come from your sharing of your family history.

As you ponder creating your legacy rather than leaving it, you may consider what activities you could incorporate family traditions. What memory-making activities could you create in the kitchen while passing along family "secret" recipes and what traditional holiday afternoon activities could you engage in at the park? A soccer game? Tree-climbing contest? Scavenger hunt?

One of our favorite family traditions is one which takes place each Thanksgiving Day afternoon. Since our five children were small, we look forward to our special time around the dining table. After the holiday meal is completed and the dishes are cleared, we spend time sharing around the table, lighting candles and laughing. Each family member is designated a certain amount of money to donate to causes that they care about. They provide background on the charities or people who will receive their portion of donated funds. This provides an opportunity for each of us to learn about new worthy recipients of our giving and share in new ways.

When our children were small, the amount of giving per person was modest, and it has continually grown over the years. The goal is to give all the funds before year's end – usually during and throughout the holiday season. It is inspiring to look back over the years and reflect on the many causes that our family has been able to help. More importantly, we created a family tradition of impacting the lives of others, which has become part of the culture and fabric of each of our children's lives.

Life Lessons

As we reflect over our experiences and consider the life lessons that we have gathered, we can collect and share our wisdom with our children and grandchildren. However, the wisdom of our learning doesn't have to be limited to sharing with our family members. Our friends, students, neighbors and employees can benefit from our life lessons as well. If you have had the experience of learning that what goes around, comes around, that's a life lesson. How we treat others will inevitably reflect upon our experiences in life. You may have helped someone in a small way, only to discover later the profound impact of your kindness.

You may have learned that delayed gratification is a good thing. In my professional experience helping hundreds of families optimize their finances, a common life lesson of successful people is that it never pays to be in a hurry when making as financial decision. When you are pressured to hurry, or act without considering each aspect of your finances, you open yourself up to making costly mistakes. Always consider the legal, investment, taxation, protective, growth angles and cash flows when implementing a financial strategy. When people rush in to buy a product, invest in the newest, hottest trend or allocate expenses, they can all-too-often learn the life lesson the hard way.

5. Take Specific Action

Your legacy is an ongoing process. Rather than a document, love letter, pile of cash or farmhouse that is gifted upon your passing.... Your Legacy is a living, breathing thing.

Consider being proactive, rather than reactive, when you are creating your legacy. This is how you can truly be rich forever. Sure, you'll want to leave some wealth, resources, money, property and business interests to your heirs; and the more the better. Consider also the wisdom you can impart to those people you care about most.

In these times, there are so many things that are outside of our control. Your legacy is something that is WITHIN your control.

Consider, when you are gone, what those who knew you will be observing in your Life Print.

Ponder the following:

Words they will say about you.

What they will learn from you.

What they will receive from you.

Wisdom they will gain from you.

So, what you can do next is this.

Spend some time reflecting on and writing down exactly what you want them to receive from you.

Money/Assets

> How much and what types of resources should they receive?

> How should they receive it?

> Should they inherit all at once, or over time?

Life lessons

> What important wisdom could they use?

> What life lessons will help them thrive?

Family heritage

> What historical, geographical, cultural family stories could you share?

> How have your ancestors shaped your life, family and occupation?

What do you want them to say about you?

The way you stay rich forever is so simple. Create your legacy. Start now!

***

To contact Judy:

www.JudyCopenbarger.com

David Chametzky

 David Chametzky is a Tedx speaker, author, mentor and podcast host of "Peace Love and Bring a Bat". "Uncle Dave" is an agent of change who is a highly authentic person that wears his heart on his sleeve. His unique perspective and passion has brought service to people searching for ways to become more empowered and wanting to level up through self-improvement.

David graduated from the University of Maryland with a Bachelor's Degree in Behavioral Sciences and has enjoyed a successful career in both the corporate and private world for close to 30 years including becoming a New York State Certified Recovery Peer Advocate.

In the journey of life we often experience a process which has been trademarked CLUBERTY(tm). This process teaches us to grow constantly by looking through the looking glass to create a positive mindset in several ways.

As a motivational speaker and mentor uses stories of rising from life's challenges and overcoming obstacles. The Phoenix Paradigm shift or through his P.A.T.H (Personal Attitude Towards Happiness) he will make sure you don't counterfeit yourself but instead become your most authentic self.

He has helped change lives of all those who have come across his path on the journey and those who join in the journey become like family of this tribe/clan.

Rise and Resilience - Igniting Your Inner Phoenix

By David Chametzky

Are you trapped? Can you figure a way out? Many of us face obstacles that we might not fully understand the challenges before us without knowing what resources might be available to us.

Let's imagine for a moment that we are all birds. Can you feel the wind in your face, the air under your wings and the sights that allow you to see forever? Now imagine this bird being the most beautiful thing you have ever seen. The bird makes sounds that are so pure touching parts of your soul and making you feel inspired. The greatness of this bird is that it enjoys all the things about life like flying, soaring to greater heights and feeling the freedom when we overcome our obstacles. The bird I want to talk to about is a bird that is so special it is mentioned in the Bible twice.

We have all been in the ashes and experienced darkness. It is often in the darkest of nights just before the sun is about to rise where we find a way to rise and find the resilience to soar again.

Knowing sadness is common among everyone and how we rise is different for each of us. Just like the Phoenix, we are reborn anew from our own ashes. There is a regrowth from the challenges and obstacles presented before us.

We find stories from all over the world which talk about this magical- mystical bird. This glorious creature can be seen building a nest and if you listen, you can hear the echoes of the melancholic song which is both sad but full of encouragement sort of like a blues song where we acknowledge the tough parts of life along with BEAUTY. We all have a song deep within ourselves that makes our hearts sing. The bird gathers everything to create a detailed pattern of branches to pebbles and it then puts it in a decorative but detailed pattern. **You can see that the creature looks fatigued, but it doesn't lessen its magnificence.** As the first rays of the sunlight peak from the horizon, the creature begins to spread its wings as if about to take flight. The features are the most perfect blend between gold and red imaginable with hues forming majestic shades. Suddenly a spark falls from the heavens, and the creature and its nest are both set on fire. Soon the creature and the nest are consumed and what lays behind are just the ashes. The Phoenix waits for the right moment in its rebirth the sun begins to rise. Can you feel the warmth of the sun and the love when things are going right?

This return to the ashes is not the end of the bird but only the beginning of the process that will continue again and again but each time allowing the bird to soar higher and higher. The process of rebirth happens every day – we all get to start anew each day and find a new pattern to move past the obstacles and ashes of the past. As the legend says after its rebirth, it then moves on to live for 1,000 years and spends those years in Heaven until the cycle restarts.

But there is nothing to worry about because the creature will rise again in its time as we are all capable to do. As it rises a song is sung and the sound rises to the heaven. **It is the sound of hope and we all know where there is hope there is life.** This bird sings –farewell song, the sun continues to rise and a spark from heaven falls and then ignites the wings of the bird. In seconds, the bird and all its beauty are turned to ashes and from there that is where the power rises because we can rebuild anew, **return to who we truly are** and find resilience that we all know we have within ourselves.

There is always a need for more than hope to rise from our ashes. Hope is the initial spark to reignite the flames within our heart.

In a descriptive sense the Phoenix is a grand bird, similar in physique with that of a peacock or an eagle. It has the most beautiful and vibrant hues of colors with blue sapphire-like eyes that shine bright in the sky. Some say that it builds a nest in the darkest hours of the night while others believe it isn't a nest but its funeral pyre. Some also believe that a spark from heaven is what sets it on fire, and some say that it is not the fire but the clapping of its grandiose wings together that causes the fire. Our bird turns its face towards the warmth of the universal love that awaits us. Whichever theory you believe the beginning and the end are the same. As it sets on fire, it turns into ashes and later is reborn again.

According to the legend, the creature never fully dies. Instead, it is reborn again and again. Just like us, we sometimes need to rise from our ashes or level up to become a better version of ourselves to soar in the clouds of resilience and growth.

I want you to think of the **Phoenix within You**.

Finding that divine spark within ourselves often needs to be reignited or directed in the right way. to achieve the greatness within ourselves.

How do I know this? I will tell you one of my truths – I am a Phoenix and I believe everyone has a Phoenix within themselves once they can see through the ashes and overcome obstacles, they believed insurmountable before.

The first time I knew I was a Phoenix was May 11, 2006. That day in 2006 I was going through a divorce. I had two girls. Life was a challenge and all I could think was my life was ending. I was sitting at this women's conference in a room filled with over a thousand people. They were high profile speakers including Madeline Albright and Geraldine Ferrero. Some serious high-profile speakers – what I experienced most is about the poem that was shared with the attendees which changed my life. Mays Angelou's poem – "Still I Rise" Now let me be straight the poem is not about the phoenix, but it does mention RISING and it was the first time this poem resonated with me. As I kept hearing about rising each breath was a struggle and then it hit me. I needed to find a way to pick myself up and learn to be **the person my children needed for me. I had to be the Phoenix for myself and my girls.** Regain the ability to RISE once more from the ashes and begin the process of resilience and regrowth. While I was going through a terrible the divorce, I realized that I needed to rise above it all and become the person. I listened to the poem more intensely I could feel new life entering my heart once again. Boom, Boom.

We all have resilience within ourselves because no matter who are at one point, we have at overcome obstacles that we didn't believe we could overcome. Ask you to think about some of the obstacles you have overcome – For example broken heart, infidelity, death of a loved one, loss of a friend, loss of a job, a care giver, or divorce. We have all experienced disappointment that we never thought we would be able to rise from. You might be experiencing some of the above experiences and feelings right now. I will tell you that once you find the right resources and use those resources than you will feel the soul of your Phoenix.

I also ask you to reach to your chest and feel that heart-beat – BOOM BOOM. That tells you that I am right, and things can change. I've been there a few times and I have learned so much from the lessons that universe was sending me. Once you find the right resource and fund those resources, then you will feel the soul of your Phoenix like I did. Remember what you give out to the universe is what you will get back.

So how do we overcome the things that we need to overcome? Each of us does it differently and not everyone is as resilient for many reasons. When we can find what is best for us and how to build better resiliency to overcome obstacles in our way. It is by digging and optimizing our brains that allows us to see how we manage situations and choose to make the decisions that will guide us. As we dig in the ashes, of our past we find so many interesting things on how we operate and why we do the things we do. Our thought patterns are created, and we adapt to the landscape that is created in. The brain is the organ that does so much for us. It runs all the background stuff like breathing but it also stores memories and is always vigilant to protect us. Some of us always operate in a state of fear when certain things happen based on past experiences. We get caught up in a cycle of thoughts. The word fear can have several meanings. Forget Everything and Run another alternative meaning being False Evidence Appearing Real. With those possible meanings of the word fear we decide it is better to run than stand and fight. Our brains are hard wired differently where decisions are made instantly based on past experiences. Just like the Phoenix the rise can happen in an instant – that magical moment when the ashes come together to form the new you. There are always possibilities and techniques used to be able to change some of the uncomfortable feelings that are stored in our memories and minds.

I will let you in on a little secret – the secret it **Between stimulus and response there is a magical space.** In that space is where decisions are made, and we can choose the right response for us. When we do not take time to build that space, we make decisions too quickly based on these past experiences. Any new task you are learning and will need to start slowly. Eventually your mind will be trained to not only learn to do that task more efficiently. An example of this is like when we learn how to type. We all started typing slowly but eventually our minds were trained to not only learn to type more quickly but also begin to type faster without even looking. That's all about training and knowing how to work through the ashes of our past to make our present more powerful. To understand the why's of our past thinking and make the present more powerful than the past.

I would never have thought about any of this in my old life but that day in May 2006 I made a decision to change my mindset from one that was geared to negative to be one of positivity. Its not as easy as one might think because of all the life ashes that were programmed throughout my life into my head. As I continued on my journey, I found out these old programs were not really as useful even though I had been doing this for such a long time. The deeper I dove into the ashes, I found reasons as to why I thought the way I did things were right and how it affected me and others around me. **Releasing the darkness within allows the spark we need to reignite our flames.** It is not as easy as one might think because of all the life programs that have been programmed into our heads.

Through my process, I personally learned how to rise for myself and to begin teaching others how to rise for themselves. There are many ways to not only heal yourself from negative experiences but to remove the triggers and in so doing life changes. It is only about getting through our pasts but knowing how to manage our futures that builds the power from within. Finding the right resources is like finding that magical spark that reignites the Phoenix from the ashes. Optimizing our brain and finding ways to overcome the negative feelings or obstacles in our way is possible.

Many of those obstacles that were created by negative experiences affected the "life filter" and changed how I saw things. As I learned my resources and showing others how to rise and overcome from their own challenges, I enjoyed seeing the faces of people who were clearing and overcoming obstacles that held them down from rising to be their best self.

In learning and then applying the skills and techniques for both myself and others, I have experienced the magic that happens. For example, if you watch a horror movie with the lights off. It can be very scary. You might hear sounds that you might have not heard before. Fear enters and we can anticipate how things are going to go. When you then turn on the lights and watch that same horror movie, it will become less scary.

I have experienced this both for myself as well as hundreds of people who have experienced very traumatic experiences such as Veterans. Once you experience relief from the ashes, we are able rise, find resilience to live very different lives.

We not only rise from past challenges, we have experienced, we also need to learn how to overcome from the past challenges, as well as the ones now before us. I once sat across from a young woman who told me that she often had panic attacks. Those panic attacks were "under control" but the ones which were not particularly, where the ones where she passed the airport or heaven forbid actually thought of getting on a plane. We began the process, and her life was changing rapidly. She actually took the chance to give us the extra added challenge of booking an international flight with her friends something she would never have thought of before. I had confidence in this amazing young woman and knew that she could overcome this. At one point she was going to give up, but she persevered. We worked together and through the decisions she made we were able to align her with the right resources and allow the right outcomes into her life. She was so prepared that when she took this life changing trip, they lost her luggage. She called me upset and as we talked, wherein that was the universes way of saying buy something new to wear during the trip. She laughed and did just that creating new memories and an opportunity to rise from her past and create a better enjoyable experience for herself. With the change of her new mindset, she was able to release the anxious feelings that she felt, was truly able to fly and allow the world really did open up for her and she was able to soar as high as she needed.

In one of Michelangelo's sonnets, the Phoenix has been used as a symbolism to portray human optimism. The poet believes that the life of the Phoenix is an inspiration to us. As the melancholic song was sang when the Phoenix began the process there is an equally powerful song as it flies in the skies. Knowing our songs help use complete the cycle with a triumphant song as we soar. The song releases from within our souls.

We are all success stories of all the things we have lived through. By living through the burning ashes and obstacles in our way and renewing ourselves with more strength, we become the best version of ourselves. Lifting ourselves out of the ashes and being revived leads to growth. We are stronger for every failure we have experienced and able to apply our learnings. We strengthen ourselves when we are able to ground ourselves. Remember the words Earth and Heart are the same letters. Grounding yourself and learning to train your brain to see the love in everything does bring your brain to resiliency and give you the ability to remove the past and enjoy the present. When you are able to reset and experience the emotional reactions and stress responses that trap your RISE then you become free. The situations and people that used to trigger your anxiety, anger or hurt no longer have any power over you. You can step forward calmly and confidently.

Whatever you experience plays a part of the process your essence through each chapter of your life. The nurturing side of myself includes many facets including that we all have a protective self but also a side where we find grace. When we feel the sad song, we need to search for the encouraging space inside ourselves to find the spark that leads to the light that brings the simplicity and clarity to fly as the Phoenix does after rising from the ashes.

Every year I celebrate my Phoenix-day – the day I really begun embracing being a Phoenix the person who chooses to rise above the challenges that have been placed before me. I also have a new definition of fear as well - FACE EVERYTHING AND RISE.

When you find your Phoenix-day and learn to Rise, finding ways to Recharge and then Return to your best self.

***

To contact David:

Website www.DavidChametzky.com.

Email: Onthepathny@gmail.com

On Facebook, Instagram, Clubhouse and Green Room as David Chametzky

Twitter as David Chametzky with the handles @goofyjaam and @onthepathny

Listen on Apple Podcasts to Peace Love and Bring a Bat. https://podcasts.apple.com/us/podcast/peace-love-and-bring-a-bat/id1552738547

Bryan Standish

Bryan Standish is a Solar Energy Consultant, Network Marketer, Real Estate Investor and Veteran of Operation Iraqi Freedom.

He has a Bachelor of Science degree from Southern Connecticut State University and has completed numerous other courses of study, including the Warrior Leader Course (WLC) while in the military and the Seasonal Law Enforcement Training Program (SLETP) in the civilian world.

Bryan is also a proud alumnus of the Tau Kappa Epsilon Fraternity. He is a charter member of both the Veterans of Foreign Wars New Haven Post 12150 and the American Legion New Haven Post 210, as well as an associate member of the Marine Corps League Peter P. Monaco Jr. Detachment 40 in Glastonbury, Connecticut.

Bryan is fascinated by all things solar, network marketing and residual income. He loves soccer, MMA and music, especially hard rock and metal.

Lessons: My First Few Years in Sales

By Bryan Standish

I was pushing 30 years old, standing in a Barnes and Noble and trying to figure out my next play. Things were not going well, to say the least, and my bank account mirrored the rest of my life.

I stood looking at all the books about improving one's financial situation, when an employee came over and asked if I needed some help. She recommended a book that would change my life forever. The book was *Rich Dad Poor Dad"* by Robert Kiyosaki. It kind of looked like a story book to me, but I got it anyway.

What I came to read completely changed my perspective and my life. That book started my journey into sales, network marketing, real estate and business. It was the catalyst for the transformation that was to take place. As one dream ended, another was soon beginning.

In the paragraphs that follow, I am going to give a brief overview of some of the most important lessons I have learned from my first few years in the solar, network marketing and real estate industries. My objective is to share the things that will have the most impact, spark the most conversation and help the most people. While many of these lessons can be used by anyone, I am especially hopeful they will make a significant impact on the young entrepreneurs and sales professionals reading this. Where possible, I will credit the people who shared this information originally and will recall details of the stories as best I can remember. I will use 'business' and 'sales' interchangeably for sake of brevity.

What is your why?

In the network marketing space, this is discussed all the time. Most people work for a paycheck, but business is a very different thing. If you do not have a clear-cut reason for *why* you are working towards building your business or sales pipeline, you are setting yourself up for certain failure. The going in any sort of entrepreneurial set up is very rough and very demanding; the numbers are not often in your favor. Get emotionally connected to what the end result of your business is. For example, do you want more freedom to spend time with your family? Or maybe you want to be able to give more money to causes that are important to you? The more of an emotional connection, and the more people you can incorporate into your why, the better. If you are just doing it for yourself, you probably won't do it at all.

The hardest person to recruit is yourself.

I was listening to network marketing trainer Rob Sperry's podcast when I first remember hearing this. It hit me hard. The most important person you have to recruit to do anything of significance is yourself. And you have to recruit yourself every day. Building a business, like any skillset, takes time. I believe this is one of the main reasons why people fail in business. They have not recruited themselves fully or enough. Recruit yourself every day, every hour if needs be. Building belief in yourself is not easy, but it is necessary. Like any other muscle it must be built over time; however, it can be lost over time too. If you can't recruit yourself, you are going to struggle to recruit and sell others on your mission.

People buy you first.

I called up the outside sales rep who was working my solar deal. The customer and I had had a great conversation in the store, and he agreed that he should take a look at solar power for his home. I set up the consultation and was excited to hear what happened after their meeting. It was a good house for solar and the customer seemed very interested.

The sales rep told me the consultation had gone alright. I was confused by the response and her tone. It had just gone "alright." This guy was all kinds of interested, why was she so unenthusiastic about this interaction. I asked her to explain. She told me that I had made a very good impression on him. This is usually a good thing in sales, I was thinking. She explained that he set the appointment because he liked me, not because he was interested in solar.

I was both flattered and confused. He was a perfect stranger. We had never met. If he had no interest, then why would he spend his time? Well, I had sold him on ME and not solar. There are several lessons here. The first of course is that being likable can get you pretty far in business sometimes. The other lesson though is that you should always give people an out. Network marketing trainer Ray Higdon talks about this a great deal, and it applies to the rest of life as well. First, ask if someone is open to receive some information, but give them an easy out if they are not—do not become attached to the results.

Looking back, I would have asked that young man some more qualifying questions to see if he was really interested in solar. Keep in mind that a solid 'no' is oftentimes just as good as a 'yes,' in that it will save you time, energy and money (maybe even an odd conversation or two with a co-worker as well).

A confused mind does nothing.

As soon as someone becomes slightly confused, the default answer is 'no.' The best salespeople are those who make things that are very confusing, simple. When I first started out, I could go on and on, talking myself right out of deals. Remember that most people can absorb very little of what you are telling them, especially if it is something they are already unfamiliar with, or worse yet, have little to no interest in.

If you have a good presentation, then use that to help keep you on track where applicable. If not, think about creating one. Perfect your pitch and learn to anticipate and answer the most frequently asked questions you encounter.

Time kills all deals.

It was just another weekly meeting for my network marketing company—at least, that is how it started. I walked into our meeting area and was shocked to see my co-worker there, the one I had been meaning to talk to for weeks about my business.

I had every intention of telling him about my business, but I did not want to be "that guy." You know, the guy who meets someone and the first words out of his mouth are about a network marketing business…their side hustle…one of those things. I had met him on literally the first day of my new solar job, and he was impressive. He had been in sales his entire adult life, pretty much, and I knew that with his business sense we could build a great business together. I mentioned to him in passing that I had some projects outside of solar moving forward on the first day we met but did not want to go into details and risk putting him off. I had every intention of following up, but I waited too long.

He had been invited to this business meeting by someone else, and while he could still join with me, it didn't feel right. I went over and greeted him, and he quickly realized that this was the other project. We talked and he was confused on why I had not asked him to take a look at the business earlier. I explained why and apologized. It was a hard lesson, but an important one.

I titled this section "time kills all deals" because if you wait too long, you will lose the deal. They will buy from someone else, join someone else, or just plain lose interest. Remember, the answer is always no if you don't ask.

Sales is a regional game.

This is what my realtor Mike Willmott told me before I bought my first investment property. His words were prophetic. My investment partners Mike and Kate Finnegan already had some real estate, and we had a great plan in place. We knew what we had to fix, how much it would cost and how to get the tenants we wanted. Well, we were right about the first two.

My business partner's other investment property was about forty minutes away. Both properties are in urban areas, right off main highways and each similar in what we knew we could get in rent. So, of course it came as shock when we were not getting any interest. Mike had been inundated with interest in his other property, yet here we were with nothing.

We finally switched up our strategy and changed our business plan, but it backed up my realtor's point. Real estate is certainly a regional game, but one that is not confined to that industry.

In my first few years in solar, I worked in numerous stores like Home Depot, Costco and BJ's. My job was to set solar appointments and help get people interested in solar power. Our management tried to sell us on the idea that all stores were created equal, but that was not quite the case.

One of the starkest examples of this was on my first day inside a Home Depot in one of Connecticut's largest cities. At first glance, it was just another Home Depot, but as soon as I started trying to communicate with the customers, I quickly realized I should have paid closer attention in Spanish class. A massive number of people could not or would not speak English. Beyond that, I realized there was a massive Brazilian population who spoke Portuguese. My knowledge of Portuguese was even less than my Spanish! This was not the start I was looking for. And to top it all off, many—if not most—people who shopped there were renters. They were instantly disqualified because in order to go solar, you must own your property.

Keep this idea of regionalism in mind when you are building your business. I recently spoke to a restaurant owner who expanded to four stores in just over two years. We started talking about customers and online ratings, and he told me a story that blew me away. He had gotten a negative review because they did not like the parmesan cheese. They WANTED the cheap imitation brand! As I smiled thinking about it, I realized that not far from that location were other places where the cheap stuff would have the business owner and his employees running for their lives!

If you aren't telling people what you do...how will they know?

I was working in a Costco one afternoon for a solar company, and we were only allowed to stand next to the exit. Pitching people especially late in the day with little interaction was not the most exciting thing in the world, especially right next to the doors in the wintertime. As I kept talking to people, one of my pitches was picked up on by someone across the aisle. Not my intended audience, but she was interested in solar and quickly made an appointment. If I had not been persistent in letting people know what my purpose was there, she probably would not have seen me, let alone heard me.

Several times have I seen people in my neighborhood go solar. It is great to see the technology spreading, but it can definitely be frustrating when you are selling that technology and losing out on your own home field, so to speak. The fact is though, most of my neighbors did not know what I do for a living. I could have gone and knocked on their door, or dropped something in their mailbox, but I did not. If you have a product or service that you believe in, you should give people the opportunity to take a look. And if you do not have a product or service you believe in, quit. Selling is a transference of belief. If you do not believe in what you are doing, you will find ways to sabotage your own success. You have to like what you see in the mirror at the end of the day.

Fortune is in the follow ups.

Darin Kidd, one of my business coaches who has made millions across several network marketing companies and franchises, recently said that 'fortune is in the follow ups.' Plural not singular. Very few deals, especially ones at the commercial level or for high-ticket items, close in one sitting. Even joining a network marketing company with low startup costs can be like this.

It took one of my friends about a year to join my network marketing company. When he finally did though, he hit the ground running and made his money back in the first few hours.

In my time in commercial solar, this was especially true. It was not unusual to have to call a business half a dozen times or more in a condensed timeframe just to get a meeting to present to them. Keep going and learn to follow up in a variety of ways—phone calls, emails, text messages, in person.

Stick and stay until you get your pay.

For those of you who do not know who Patrick Bet David is, I highly encourage you to look him up. He a Christian refugee from Iran who made his way to America during the 1980s, was a perpetual underachiever, joined the US Army, and after serving, went into sales—eventually starting his own company. One of the things he points out is that the most successful people spend years and years, often decades and decades, in the same field. I see a lot of hopscotching around today. It is hard to get to know an industry or hone a specific set of skills when you are constantly changing. I have been guilty of this in the past. Become proficient at one or two industries to start, and then branch out later.

Multiple streams of income.

When I first started down the road of sales and business, I kept coming upon this idea of having multiple streams of income. According to statistics, the average millionaire has seven streams of income. My goal was to try and replicate this. My thinking was something like this: "Well, I am already involved in solar and network marketing. Let's do real estate. That is three. What about affiliate marketing? Yes, that could be good. Oh yeah, a part-time job would be good. Plus, these other projects are taking some time to build, and I need some money now. Getting another certification could be useful too…" And on it went.

I spent a great deal of time early on trying to do too many things across too many different business opportunities. Yes, there are many people who have several successful businesses, for sure, but almost all of them start out by building one into a success first, then branching out. I failed to understand that early on.

A man convinced against his will is of the same opinion still.

When I first got into sales, I thought that a good salesman could and should be able to sell to anyone and everyone. The truth is that if a person does not want to buy, they won't. It doesn't matter how great the value or the price point at which you offer it or how big the problem is that your service or product fixes. There is a plethora of reasons for this. You may not be the right person to deliver the message, or they may not be in the right place in their lives to hear it. Many times, I have had people respond to my pitch as they are walking out the door with something that is just not true. "I don't want to rent the panels" …"It's a scam"…etc. Work with the willing and meet people where they are.

You make up in numbers what you lack in skill or…

It has been said that sales is a numbers game. It has also been said that you can make up for in numbers what you lack in skill. While I don't disagree, I would add that you can also make up for in numbers what your potential audience lacks in their understanding of your product or service—OR what they lack in their urgency to make a buying a decision. This should be remembered, because as mentioned before, the fortune is in the follow ups. And if you are in a new/er or misunderstood industry, this is even more important to keep in mind.

What people think of you is none of your business.

Developing a thick skin is important, but not easy. As an entrepreneur, you are going to face many people who do not believe in you or your business. And its not the strangers that hurt you the most, it's the people you know, who's opinions you care about. 'People do not believe a prophet in their own backyard,' it has been said. There is a lot of truth to that, but you are not alone in your struggles; everyone chasing a big goal has been through it. Remember that change is painful, change is the death of self, and whether that is you evolving as an entrepreneur or a potential customer trying to evolve out of outdated ideas or beliefs, the waters can be rough. Ships are safe in the harbor, but that is not what they are built for.

Go forward and do great things!

I wish you luck and look forward to connecting with you!

***

bryanstandish@sbcglobal.net

https://www.linkedin.com/in/bryanstandish/

Julie Rivera

Julie was born and raised in small town Canada when life took her on a journey and is now currently residing in Texas. She has had over a decade of experience serving and teaching others in various roles. Julie is the founder of Coaching with JulZ. She has always been motivated to gain a deeper awareness around the thoughts, feelings, and behaviors of others. Julie is a certified Health and Life coach. She has an undergraduate degree in Psychology and a Master's degree of Science in Marriage, Couple, and Family Counseling specializing in Trauma and Crisis. This resulted in her quest to find her true calling in coaching focusing on Mindset Transformation. Julie has taken charge of her life and discovered how to get unstuck and become the creator of a life she desires. Her passion is to serve others, to teach how to align the mind and body as one, therefore cultivating her practice.

Julie is a co-host of a podcast with her daughter called Our Chic Chat. They have an open discussion of life to embrace the laughter and struggles along the way.

Julie understands what it takes to make changes in self and has ultimate compassion for her clients as they embark on their own journey to self-discovery.

How to Discover your Best Self from a Flipped House

By Julie Rivera

Imagine standing in the kitchen on a regular day of your life and feeling the same contentment as you did the day before, somewhere in between fine and indifferent. Then all of a sudden, this tremendous force comes and flips your house upside down; as you look around after slowly getting back on your feet, nothing is as it was before. Let me be clear in reality; hindsight is always 20/20. Looking back, I had many signals that gave me clear signs my house was about to flip. I just chose to keep my eyes closed in hopes I could avoid the apparent significant change that was about to be upon me.

To give you a bit of context of the past, I felt like I did what society told me to do in life. I was married and had my beautiful children. My days were filled with loving the moments when my kids were kids; laughter and playful banter **filled** the walls. I submerged myself into all of my roles so well, especially as a parent, that when I went to any social event, and I didn't have the kids to "hide" behind, I almost didn't know how just to be myself. The roles I hid behind were being a mom, wife, and professional. Other than that, I didn't see the core of who I was.

I ignored everything that made me uncomfortable and pushed it all inside this box at the back of my brain. I just had no idea that the box was almost at capacity and was about blow.

The top of the box blew, and I was standing amid a new divorce. My children were older, and they didn't need me the way they did in their younger years. Here I am; I had no idea who the "I am" was. It was dark, and I wasn't sure what the future held for me as I was in my 40s and what I thought I wanted for my life was no longer on the table. Little did I know I was about to get this party started! Sitting with myself was the hardest and the best decision or gift I have ever made for myself. When positive changes began to happen for me, and I stepped out as a new confident "out of my shell" self, my long-time friend asked if I was going through a midlife crisis.

My answer was, if all of this greatness is a midlife crisis, then I am a big YES!

I had to dig deep and tap into what it was that fueled me? Who was I without the external world around me? Validating me for the role I played. Once I reframed my mindset on life that happened FOR me and not TO me, it changed the game. I began to visualize who I wanted to become without the mind's filter or the "how" this could happen. With my feet planted on the floor, my body relaxed, and my eyes closed, I allowed the images to flow. I connected to my five senses and noticed everything from what sounds I would hear to the color of nail polish on my fingers. What was I feeling? This version of myself felt free, independent, and was light. I was smiling all the while feeling absolute peace. Now how exactly do I get there?

With a degree in Psychology and a Master's in Counseling, it was clear I love to serve, so that was my starting point. I invested in coaching to help me identify the action steps to uncover which direction I wanted to go. Along this journey, I have identified and obliterated the obstacles that kept me stagnant for too long. I have reclaimed my own life and found a sense of peace that is truly priceless. I have taken my educational background and life experience to become a Mind and Body Integration Coach to ultimately help others reclaim and take charge of their own lives.

That brings me to the question. Why is change so hard? Why does our conscious mind allow us to dream change, but when push comes to shove, we choose to stay in our comfort zones?

Fear can feel like a paralysis within the mind and body, making change seem like the impossible for some. This feeling can keep us unintentionally stuck in a loop. When we think about our own technology devices, we get these alerts to update our operating system to the latest version. The software update allows the device to function at its best. What would it feel like if we got the alert that it was time to update our thought patterns? Unfortunately, we do not receive notifications as quickly as our devices. However, on the outside we are looking like we are the best versions of oneself, but the constant narrative that runs through our brains is operating as the outdated version. We can determine if we are using an out-of-date system by measuring our habits and behaviors and the old belief system we have hung onto since childhood. We will typically get the notification it's time to update when we start to feel unwell in our mind, body, and soul.

We desperately want to change but do not always recognize the one thing that is standing in the way of getting what we want. Our **SELF** is what is getting in the way. The story we like to tell ourselves is that we have done everything to change, but for some reason, we can't seem to move forward, staying in stuck mode. We fail to realize that doing more of the same is simply going to produce the result of more of the same. If you want different, you have to do and be different. You have to expand yourself to hold the new. This can only occur when you put action behind the desire. It doesn't matter how many times you fall, what counts is how many times you are willing to get back up and do it again.

Brains like to analyze, generalize, and distort. This is what it does unapologetically; it is not uncommon to tell the brain this "thing or dream" cannot be done because *what if?* The negative *what-if* question sequence can be the thief of joy. *What if* doing something for me makes me feel like I am neglecting my family, or I feel doing something that I am doing what I want, then it brings feelings of guilt? *What if* I am successful and I cannot keep it? If we stick in that spiral phase, it is no wonder why it seems scary to try something new. To every **ONE** thing, there are always two sides. To every fear of what could go wrong, there is a possibility it could go right. I like to refer to this as flipping the script.

Flipping the script shows the other side of the *what-if* question, such as *what if* we are leading the family to value themselves by teaching that self-care is essential. Allowing one to nurture the desire and passion within causes healthier and happier relationships with friends and family. *What if* this shows the younger generation to go for the opportunities and not be afraid to take chances? Reframing the thoughts will begin to loosen these restraints, which have unintentionally been the reason to remain stagnant for far too long.

Have you ever had this feeling that there is something more, but you can't put your finger on it? There are ways you can begin to discover what your biggest desire is and how to start taking steps toward that version of you best self you can start to see. It is time to stop playing into everything else and start bringing yourself forward into YOUR life. In no way am I downplaying the role of your profession, being a parent, or a spouse. The big message is DO NOT forget about YOU.

There is no time like the present moment to start your journey of self-discovery. Get a notebook and Journal thoughts of what ignites you. Write like no one is watching, and do not overthink; just let the words flow. You should begin to see a pattern unfold. Is it creativity? Do you want to be an entrepreneur or simply travel and blog? Next, you may want to download an audible book or build your library from people who have already done it and wrote about their journey. There is no one you can learn more from in the world than the people who can say, "been there done that."

Social media can be a great resource and is literally at our fingertips to network with others. There are groups for everything, and if you cannot find a group, I challenge you to create one. I was always told leaders go first! Do not be afraid to talk about your desire with a supportive someone and create that momentum. Hearing yourself discuss what excites you helps build up the creative energy and is exhilarating.

The first step is complete, and you have begun to uncover what you would like to do or become. In this phase, awareness is the key to it all, and once you become aware of the external and internal blocks, there is no going back. The process is an essential part of this journey. I need to remind you that this process is about understanding that you are your hero and letting go of seeking the validation of others is paramount. You have and are all that you need, as the answers are internal. You need to be your own advocate to be the best version of yourself.

How often will people say that they cannot start a business or live out a dream until this or that happens? Life will always show up and give you a million reasons why the timing is off, or one should wait. If you wait, will you remember what ignited that passion? The pressure to live under these roles of spouse, parent, and career can be overwhelming and take up a lot of space in the mind. We do not often stop and consider that you should also be making sure time is spent nourishing your soul. Taking care of others first tends to come naturally and is the road we take first without a second thought. Taking care of oneself is where we tend to fall short; we unintentionally neglect the one mind, body, and soul that will be with us for life. One day the time will come, and the kids are older, and the relationship with self is strained or unknown. No one to hide behind could feel like being picked up and placed somewhere in the middle of nowhere with a stranger.

I learned many lessons from when my house flipped upside down, but the one that was the million-dollar lesson for me was one my children let me in on. Since I have begun to be more transparent, learn new things, and dream big by becoming my own boss, they have been brave enough to do the same in their own lives, starting to take chances and be who they are without fear.

Kids do not learn from what you say, they learn from what you do. So, by keeping my box tucked away and not being authentic to myself, that is what my children were learning. Once I decided to live life on my terms and flip my house back up, I saw immediately how my whole family dynamic changed. My mini adults have begun to step out of their comfort zones. They have started to talk about following their dreams and not being afraid to be who they are. It was a massive awareness for me as a mother because of my pride. I was afraid to step out as my authentic self and was unintentionally showing them to do the same.

We can safely say that it was selfish for me to set my dreams aside and not be transparent with that side of me or not pursue the business venture. As I mentioned earlier, there are two sides to everything. In my head, putting others first was the most unselfish thing I could do. Once you are aware, you will see that you show up positively to everyone around you personally and professionally.

I had a passion for starting my own coaching business because of my flipped house, and the feeling of true peace and happiness is something that I want to ignite in others. To find their voices and let them know they are the creator of their life; it all starts with a desire.

When I heard the word coaches, I would automatically think of sports. In a way, they are similar as we cheer you on, support, and give you the skills to practice what you are learning. Knowing the foundation of what I wanted my business to be based on, it was easy to come up with these five paradigms.

1. How you do one thing is how you do everything. If you are meeting resistance or distracted in one area of life, how is it showing up in other areas?

2. Challenges are people's greatest gifts.

3. No such thing as FAILURE, only FEEDBACK. Experiences provide the necessary feedback, allowing momentum to continue or change the direction.

4. Progress over Perfection. Perfection is subjective, and if you wait for the time to be perfect, it could be years or not at all.

5. View the thoughts that come in with curiosity and NOT judgment.

These foundational principles are the bases needed to invoke the forces of change from the inside! Once you are aware of what drives the thoughts and behaviors, it is life changing. Then you will be able to make the conscious choice to change the channel on those negative or unwanted thoughts per se that are keeping you in that stuck loop or better yet not operating on the updated system.

Now that you are aware of the ways to start digging deep into your own desire for self let us talk about how to step into this as a daily routine. Even if you have not quite come to the conclusion as to the direction you would like to go starting your day off with a positive mindset can genuinely impact yourself and interactions as you go about your day. There is this sweet spot as you are waking up from your sleep when your mind is not inundated with your daily to do list. Do not reach for your phone or turn on the news take a few minutes to prime the mind of gratitude. All of the notifications of the day and emails will still be there. Give yourself the gift of setting yourself up for taking charge of YOUR day.

I have come across many ways to start the day, and you have to work with what is best for you. Think of yourself as a science lab, and it may not go in the order of what I am saying or someone else, but you try a little of this and a little of that until you find what works for you. We can get overwhelmed with the power of suggestion and forget it is only a suggestion.

I will always be a lifelong learner, but I have recently grasped to take what resonates with who I am as a coach and an entrepreneur and let the rest go.

Here are some tips to start shifting mindset immediately.

1. **GRATITUDE:** Before your feet hit the floor in the morning, start journaling, or make a mental list of everything you are grateful for. Taking time for gratitude is also great for a midday reminder if you are feeling tension. 60 seconds is all it takes.

2. **INTENTION:** Set the intention word of the day. As an example, your intention word could be I will remain in a **calm** state at work, or I will be **intentional** with everything that I do today.

3. **ACTIVITY:** Start the day with movement to include stretches, walk, or anything that gets the body moving.

4. **ACTION:** Have a goal/ dream you want to accomplish then take an action step toward making it happen. Create momentum!

Do not allow the illusion of fear to paralyze the mind and body into staying stagnant in life. Change can be undoubtedly uncomfortable, but that discomfort means growth.

A flipped house doesn't mean chaos forever; it is a reminder that it is time to grow. We rarely talk about exponential personal growth without being confronted by a problem or an issue first. Remember, the most beautiful rainbows come after the storm.

***

To contact Julie:

www.coachingwithjulz.org

https://www.instagram.com/coachingwithjulz/

https://www.facebook.com/groups/333604694631597

http://linkedin.com/in/julie-rivera-1028b381

coachingwithjulz@gmail.com

Podcast

Our Chic Chat can be found on Spotify and Apple Podcast

https://open.spotify.com/show/5eIMBAoxwLBmy71Fn3kWyq?si=
YpMi-tEnRh2d6-tKcd3cmQ&dl_branch=1

Tara L. Killen

As a Certified Life Mastery Consultant, Tara Killen can help you design and manifest a life that's in harmony with your Soul's purpose. For over 5-years Tara has worked with professionals, helping them build their dreams, accelerate their results, and create richer, more fulfilling lives. As a sought-after life coach and professional speaker Tara offers inspiring workshops to sold-out audiences around the country as well as transformational in-depth coaching programs that help clients achieve new heights of success, meaning, and spiritual aliveness.

Now combining this background with the proven DreamBuilder technology, Tara is helping clients achieve extraordinary results in accelerated time. She is filled with joy and gratitude as she works with people to transform their lives and close the gap between the life they were living and the life they LOVE living.

Tara offers content rich interactive workshops that take participants on a journey in which they design, define, test, and experience a crystal-clear vision of the life they would love – a life that is in alignment with their highest purpose. They will have a unique opportunity to "step into" the life they are imagining and feel a resounding "yes".

Success – The Real Secret

By Tara L. Killen

What if I told you that there is nothing you can **do** to be successful?

What if I told you that everything I did to become successful didn't work until I learned the secret sauce that brings all the recipes together?

The truth is… this chapter contains the part about success and cracking the rich code that, up until now, has been left out.

The Beginning

I spent the early part of my life trying to figure out how life works. We all listen to adults around us, religious leaders, people on different media, and to our peers in search of the answers to life and all its mysteries. We imitate those whom we see as having the answers and stumble through life trying to get hurt as little as possible. We build relationships of various kinds, do the best that we can, and try to succeed in work, making as much money as we think we can. If you are anything like me, you have been searching for the people in the know who have things figured out, which is why you are reading this book right now.

What we're told:

I believed that:
- Money doesn't grow on trees
- Money is the root of all evil
- All rich people are arrogant and selfish
- It is better to give than to receive
- You must work hard to make a living
- Only a tiny percentage of people in the world can have all the world's wealth
- Some things aren't meant to be
- The universe likes to mess with people
- We can't afford that ("that" equaling anything more than what we currently have)

- It is better to just accept what you have rather than to rock the boat and risk losing it all

Most of us can agree that we have all heard these statements a time or two and, if we really look at our beliefs, most of us have integrated this way of thinking into our own way of thinking. We accept these things and others like them as absolute truths. The reality is, they are not true at all.

The truth:
- Money is made of paper and paper comes from trees
- Money is the symbol of our own freedom. Greed is the root of all evil.
- People who perceive themselves as poor can be arrogant and selfish, just like those they perceive as wealthy. Most wealthy people I have encountered in this life are down to earth, extremely generous.
- If you give and never receive, you will have nothing left to give. The universe abhors a vacuum. If you set up regular giving with gratitude, you must receive. Accept when abundance comes, however small, to get the flow going.
  - A fire burns after you give it wood, and in kind, abundance will come after giving to others first. No one says to the fire, give me heat and I will give you wood. We regularly say that when I have more money, I will then give to others. Give now and give thanks for what you do have; do not think in line with lack. Giving with a lack mindset will manifest lack. By giving with a grateful heart, being thankful for the abundance you have right now, more abundance will come your way.
- Two hard working people can have the same career. One succeeds while the other fails. Working hard is **not** what decides success.
- We talk about wealth in "piece of the pie" percentages so that people can have an image in their minds. The truth is, there is no limit to wealth and abundance. It is not finite. The circle of the pie does not close.

Simply, although your perception may be that there is a limit to how much abundance a person can have, there is **no** limit. The snapshot we are shown of the **current** wealth distribution on a pie graph shows a small percentage of people having most of the wealth. That image shows **what exists now**, *not* what is possible. You can have abundance without taking anything away from anyone else.

- Thinking that succeeding or being rich is not meant to be is like a bird thinking it is not meant to fly when it is a fledgling.
- God, some divine entity, or the universe itself does not mess with people. It is, however, true that we have a curriculum in this life to learn from and we have free will as to how we respond to all curriculum we encounter in our lives. There is no inherent good or bad in that curriculum, there are just situations. We energetically charge them when we decide if they are good or bad, giving them an energetic vibration in our lives. It is also true that our outer life reflects the thoughts we hold in our inner life.
- We maintain invisible boundaries which keep us from attaining what we desire. Once we realize that, we can choose to remove them.

How do we live a life we love? What is the Rich Code?

In short… Decision.

Let me explain:
- Have you ever started the day by dribbling toothpaste down the front of your shirt and then everything went wrong for the rest of the day?
- Have you ever started on a road trip hoping for it to go well with the drivers you would encounter being skillful and courteous, yet was prepared for them to be oblivious and unskilled? Did you notice you encountered oblivious and unskilled?
- Have you ever used your imagination to think about what might happen in a situation, dwelled on it replaying it in your mind, and had it come true?

- Have you ever had a wonderful morning and everything during the rest of that day went wonderfully?

In each of these situations, unbeknownst to you, **you** decided. You had certain thoughts, which created certain physical responses and emotions. Those responses and emotions had a certain expectation and vibration.

- In the 1st scenario, when you dribbled the toothpaste, I bet you thought that the day sucked already. Toothpaste on your shirt is not good or bad, it is just toothpaste that happens to be on your shirt. By assigning negative thoughts to the situation, (a decision was made), which evoked emotional and physical responses, you effectively decided that the day sucked. In doing that, you set up that expectation, backed it with a negative vibration, and the universe gave you what you were in that moment. More matches to your vibration.

- In the 2nd scenario, unknowingly an emotionally charged expectation, (a decision was made), was established by being prepared for the worst. You hoped for skillful and courteous, but really expected oblivious and unskilled. You were prepared for the worst, hence was a vibrational match for the worst, and got exactly that.

- In the 3rd scenario, imagination was used to create a future scenario, (a decision was made), and then when it came true, it had been expected. People all the time say, "See…. I told you that was going to happen!" When we create a scenario in our mind and re-live it repeatedly, we are evoking emotions, changing our vibration, holding an expectation, and giving a blueprint of what we want to experience. Can you imagine what would happen if you used your powers for good???

- In the 4th scenario, when the morning goes well, we often have a good day, (a decision was made), if we maintain that vibration. We tend to hold a positive outlook, use our imagination for good, and expect a good day.

We are more powerful than we know. This is how:

We all, in general, have a memory, right? Essentially, we look back at life lived and see the past in our mind's eye.

Did you know that you have memory that works forward in time? It is called imagination.

When you imagine something, your body does not know it is not yet factual and reacts just as if you are looking back at memories. Have you ever imagined something exhilarating and your heart races? Have you ever imagined a situation going badly and you feel a knot in your stomach or fear rushing through your body? These examples are proof that your body thinks that what you are imagining is really happening now!

The truth is…. Your thoughts become things. This is how:

When you think something, there is an emotion that associates with that thought. That emotion is at a certain energetic vibration, which changes depending on what the thought is. In this life, like attracts like. What that means is, we do not get what we want, we do not get what we do, rather we attract WHO WE ARE! **This** is the Law of Attraction that you hear so much about. We are going to talk more about the immutable laws of the universe a little later.

So many times, people expect the worst, but want the best. We see and feel all the ways something can go wrong repeatedly, and then say, "See, I told ya so!". Many times, I have heard people say, "I am just not meant to be XXXXX" where XXXXX is anything positive like being happy, wealthy, or married, etc.

Let me ask you this…. When was the last time you flipped the light switch on in a house and when the lights didn't come on you said to yourself, "Well, I guess I am not meant to have light."? The answer is, YOU DON'T! When the electricity isn't working, you know it is a transmission problem…that for one reason or another the electricity is not flowing to your house, or that switch. The exact same answer is true when your life is not reflecting what you would love. You must fix the flow of energy…. the way you think, what you feel, and what you *truly* expect to happen. We must reflect deeply and be honest with ourselves, not defensive, telling ourselves stories. Rationalizing will *never* help you manifest what you would love.

You have heard people reference the bible quote that the road to hell is paved with good intentions, right? You have also likely heard the quote from the bible that the kingdom of heaven is within you. Those directly correlate here. If you want A, (your *intention*), and your *attention* is on B, the result is going to be B. Many say it this way.... Energy flows where attention goes. A few possible examples:

- The intention is to have a well-behaved dog
  - o Attention during free time is given to social media instead of working with the dog
- The intention is to build a business
  - o Attention is given to TV, what might prevent the business, why it is hard, and doing other things instead of taking whatever step can be taken to start building the business
- The intention is to have a committed spouse and share a life together
  - o Attention is given to what feels good in the moment instead of things like making room in the house for another person to share the space or taking the steps that would be taken if that committed person were already here.
- The intention is to be wealthy
  - o Attention is given to what you can't see in the right now, creating a vibration of lack.

Is that all there is to it?

The high-level formula to manifest a life you would love, as explained here in this chapter, is a simple one. There are also nuances to the formula that are at play. These nuances are based in who we are and how we interact with the immutable laws of the universe. These nuances are why cracking the rich code seems easy for some people and hard for others. This chapter is not long enough to go into deep detail; however, it certainly can give you a basic understanding.

First let's start with the immutable laws of the universe.

There are invisible, immutable laws of the universe at play every second of every day. Just as electricity was until it was understood and utilized to our advantage, these laws exist and are waiting to be used by you.

You have heard the expression, "It doesn't work unless you work it"? Unless the laws of the universe are used, the benefits they can bring are not seen. We sometimes trip into using these laws and do not realize it. We later try to repeat the creation of a certain outcome, not knowing that a law of the universe was utilized to begin with, and then have difficulty understanding why the outcome was not repeatable. Often superstition then comes into play where we feel that the universe/God/some outside force or entity is messing with us or punishing us or we are not meant to have/experience something.

There are many laws, however this chapter will only cover three of them.

- The 1st of these three laws has already been covered. That law is the Law of Attraction.
  - o In short, you don't get what you want, you don't get what you do, you get what you are.
- The 2nd law we are going to cover is the Law of Increase
  - o In short, whatever you praise will increase. This will be covered in deeper detail below.
- The 3rd and final law we are going to cover is the Law of Forgiveness
  - o I have chosen this law to close out the chapter because of how intertwined it is in manifesting the life we would love living as well as our overall wellbeing

The Law of Increase

Some also call the Law of Increase the Law of Praise. When you praise something or someone, you lift your consciousness upward and open yourself up to receive all the good headed your way. Everything and everyone will respond to praise. Have you ever heard that what you resist persists? Stop complaining and start applying the use of praise to your self-confidence, your body, to people you are going to meet with, to your waitress or waiter, to drivers on the road with you, to money, to family, to employees, and the list goes on.

Some examples of the law in action:

Have you ever heard that talking nice to your plants every day helps them grow better? Something even more compelling...Have you ever heard of Dr. Masaru Emoto? Dr. Emoto's experiments involved labeling bottles of water with various words, then freezing the water and examining the frozen crystals under a microscope. The results were that positive words on the water produced beautiful crystals, while negative words produced ugly crystals. Here is a link to a video with pictures of Dr Emoto's results. (I do not necessarily advocate or oppose anything in this video. It is purely for you to see photos of the results yourselves.) https://youtu.be/lUIJjiQCV34 This is a link to a double-blind study that was done later using the same hypothesis in the original experiments: https://pubmed.ncbi.nlm.nih.gov/16979104/.

The Law of Forgiveness

Forgiveness is defined as a conscious, deliberate decision to release feelings of resentment or vengeance toward a person or group who has wronged you, regardless of whether they deserve your forgiveness. Notice that in this definition it says nothing of condoning, excusing, or forgetting. Forgiveness is also a life practice, not a one and done thing. You may even feel that it is a lie when you first forgive. When you truly forgive a person or group who has wronged you, what you are doing is releasing yourself from maintaining a prison in your mind. You are freeing yourself from feelings and emotions that are harmful to you.

As mentioned above in different ways, thoughts become things. An example given above is that words and emotions can impact the crystalline structure of water when frozen.

- Harboring the feelings of resentment or vengeance and being the jail keeper of your mind hurts you, not them.
- Disease in the body is an energy problem and a lack of forgiveness eats away at you. Think of it as Dis – Ease.
- The laws of physics tell us that we are made up of protons, neutrons, electrons, etc. and those particles break down into smaller particles of energy.
  - If we are simply energy, why would we ever allow anything into our lives that reduces our energetic vibration?

    o   Forgiveness releases you from the energy jail and raises your vibration, not the offenders.

The book, "A Course in Miracles" by Helen Schucman describes it as "Forgiveness is a shift in perception that removes a block in me, to my awareness of love's presence."

Next, let's talk about who we are:

We are all born and have people who raise us. During our upbringing, we have genetic pieces in play, and environmental pieces in play. These puzzle pieces come together to create the operating system by which we function, judge all things, and make decisions. Some parts of our operating systems are in alignment with the immutable laws of the universe, and some are not. How aligned someone is varies from person to person. These puzzle pieces also try to determine for us how much happiness, success, abundance, romance, adventure, etc. we are going to allow into our lives. Our operating system creates boxes for every life category you can think of with different height ceilings for us to live within, depending on the category. If we don't realize that our current operating system is doing this, we often live the same life year after year as opposed to living a growth filled life every year. This is often most easily explained as giving up great for good. Good is the biggest murderer of great. Because of our operating system creating a subconscious ceiling of safety for us, we tend to give up great because whatever we are looking at in life is good enough. Essentially, we are willing to live with what may suck because it is good enough and we don't want to challenge our operating system.

The ceilings created by our operating system are also known as limiting beliefs or negative paradigms. These once served us, however it is our responsibility to recognize them and ask ourselves if they still serve us. Are they holding us back from great? From what we would love?

Invisible walls are sometimes less than invisible... as in they don't exist except in our own limiting beliefs or operating system. In short, sometimes it is doing the thing or getting the thing that holds us back from achieving or attaining it, not our inability to do or get it at all.

In a nutshell...

From start to finish, in a nutshell, the secret sauce for cracking the rich code lies within you. You alone have the power to observe how you are reacting in situations and have the power to choose what your reaction will be. You alone have the power to decide what kind of life you are going to live. Are you going to live a life in which you are the conductor or are you going to live a life based on other people's decisions? You alone manifest the life experience you have. You alone chose to follow or ignore the laws of the universe.

Always remember... you are much more powerful than you know. I coach people from all walks of life, and that is key to you cracking your rich code. I wish you all the success the world can bring and hope that this chapter has brought you at least a glimmer of your own potential.

***

To contact Tara:

Web site: Https://tarakillen.lifemasteryconsultant.com/

Appt Link: http://calendly.com/tarakillen_lifemasteryconsultant

Email: info@inspirationdiscoverystore.com

Rhonda Grant

Rhonda Grant is a true renaissance woman. Co-founder and CEO of Stand Fast Homes Ltd., and Grant's Marble Inc., she is an active leader and highly regarded as an award-winning real estate professional.

Abruptly, a near-death experience fractured her everyday routine, compelling Rhonda to author her book, *Magical Forces Within: Extraordinary Discoveries in an Ordinary Life. This dynamic exploration of the metaphysical inspires her readers with real-life stories of transformation and enlightenment.*

Rhonda is a Radio Talk Show Host with Contact Talk Radio Network. Her Podcast: *The Rhonda Grant Show*, is part of the C-Suite Network, where Rhonda is an Executive Leader and Contributor.

Time

by Rhonda Grant

The moment you were born someone noted the time, recorded your arrival and acknowledged your existence. Time, day, and year matter astrologically because of where the planets sat at the moment you arrived. Apparently, this is what determines most of the events in your life. You were born somewhere along your evolutionary path, and you, just like the rest of us, are conditioned to acknowledge and adhere to the most important aspect of life — time.

Time is everywhere — on your phone, computer, vehicle, and billboards. It reminds you if you are running late or are exactly where you are meant to be at that moment. Time is so important a whole industry was born of clocks and watches. "Am I late, early, or on time? I need to know if I need to hurry up, be angry with people who will not hurry up, even yell at those who will not move faster. People are waiting — what will they think if I am late? I must be on time!"

It is Tuesday morning, September 11th, 2001, in New York City, with its hustle and bustle. People are getting their kids off to school and daycare. Some are trying to inhale their morning coffee. The person waiting in line at Starbucks is watching the clock, because the customer ahead of them cannot decide what type of coffee they want. Could this delay in a person's ordinary routine that seems common yet alters one's course and spares their life?

When you consider time from this perspective and acknowledge the lives that were spared because they were running late that morning — the power of the thought may give you pause. Sometimes, the universe has a way of stalling you, putting obstacles in your way to slow you down – but many of us ignore these intuitive hits, because we have a commitment which includes being somewhere at a specific time. How could anyone know they were rushing to their death? Perhaps they had a bad feeling — a voice from their unconscious urging them to slow down. But it wasn't loud enough to slow them down, so they could avoid the unknown disaster looming ahead.

I remember speaking with a man who had the same last name as my mother's maiden name. He was a manager in a cheese factory. For some reason, we started talking like we were old friends and he told me that because his great-grandfather was running late, he missed boarding the Titanic. The strangest feeling came over me at that moment, because had time worked differently on that fateful day, the man before me may not have been born. A whole family line would never have existed, and no one would know it was missing. I often wonder if those who heed their inner voice, and slow down – – or make a different decision — are sometimes spared harm.

Time has given us our history, which we have turned into a story, based on our own interpretations of the tales told to us, and the stories we tell ourselves about ourselves. Sometimes, when we reflect on specific moments in our past, we find we are still gripped with the pain from what we experienced, or from our own transgressions against others. Time cannot change that; we need to gather our own bravery to address our issues and allow ourselves time to heal those parts of us that need nurturing. But there are those of us who do not have the courage to face the pain again, even if it is to heal. We carry it with us instead, letting it infringe on our time with others. It shows up in our conversations when we hear not what is said, but rather what we interpret from what is said.

Meanwhile, we feel as if we are in control of our lives — that we've got this. Yet often we are out of control because we do not have a crystal ball to know what comes next. Consider the wake-up call we received when the pandemic arrived, and a lockdown was declared. It seemed as if overnight, our world completely changed. We shifted our vision of time and what time meant. How long will this last? Will my company survive? Will I have a job when this is over? Workplaces, daycares, schools, clubs, fitness, sports activities, and restaurants, all closed. Other places like seniors' homes locked down, because of the high number of COVID-19 cases and deaths. Our roads and streets became eerily quiet. What would the fall-out be because of it? Our time was compartmentalized into days, weeks, and then months. We had to wait another week to see what our leaders would decide, about when our economy could re-open. It would be either more time in isolation or returning to a new normal.

Most people lived in fear, because we were bombarded with media, depicting what was going on in other countries. It seemed as if we were living in a Stephen King novel. Each day we listened to rising statistics about virus cases and deaths all over the world, and it was frightening.

Many people reverted to their reptilian brains; the survival genes kicked in. There were shortages at stores, as people began to hoard food and supplies. Some bought baby chicks, because they matured quickly and could produce eggs, creating an ongoing food source for a family. Gun owners bought ammunition. The uncertainty of the pandemic affecting the food chain scared people, and they wanted to be able to hunt, if need be. It was a way of tucking-in, and people setting up for the long haul. The lack of distractions – local and national sports, theatres, dinners, and in-person school, made us feel like we were living in heavily restricted ghost towns, villages, and cities.

Some people did not fare well in isolation because they could not see their loved ones. Some were waiting on a surgery they needed and found that the procedure was constantly booked, cancelled, and rebooked because hospitals were taking care of those stricken by the pandemic.

It is interesting to observe that as time moved on, people became desensitized to the media's fearful language and predictions. When the second and third waves of the virus hit, people looked for hope instead. When would a vaccine be available? We learned quickly that making plans did not mean they were going to happen, because even though schools, restaurants, and businesses were open today, there was no certainty about tomorrow.

What has the pandemic taught us about time? For many, we learned to reprioritize things — we learned to do without what we previously felt we could not live without. Time changes our perspective, and during a pandemic, we all worked on finding ways to speed it up. We hoped that the development of a vaccine would hurry up, so we would feel safe, see our loved ones, and go to work again. We wanted to see our children back in school. We concerned ourselves with how this would affect them in the long run.

When people stayed home, they learned how to do business differently. They were forced into a different type of survival. They allowed more time for personal creativity because there was no longer a commute to work. The entrepreneurial spirit that had lain dormant within many, rose, giving light to a new excitement about the future and the possibilities therein. People who spent time in creative thought birthed books, poetry, and songs. Pictures were painted, gardens were planted, and animal husbandry began. People spent time meditating and began to get in touch with their inner selves.

We never know when a regular check-up with the doctor may end up with a series of tests and a diagnosis that our days, weeks, or months are limited. Is there an opportunity to consider how we spend our time before we are told that our time here is limited?

What happens when we do not take care of the things that need tending, when we run out of time and the project is not completed, or when we choose not to address an issue that needs addressing, hoping it goes away? Time has a way of showing you just how big the little things can get, by increasing the cost associated with the unresolved issue. If you reflect on these situations and then step forward, show up and pay attention to what needs to be taken care of, time takes care of the rest. Perhaps not in a way you intended, but in a way that reflects the mindset from which you approached the situation. In that moment, you might curse and acknowledge the "I should have," or you might simply not take responsibility at all. Other words for responsibility are action and attention. They speak to one's ability to take immediate action when it is possible to correct the situation. When you do not act, you have only yourself to reckon with – and not time. Stop trying to negotiate with yourself, and with time.

Hold yourself in the highest esteem possible, so you can benefit from time. Mold time into what you want your reality to be. You are the creator of yourself and your circumstances. Believing otherwise is cheating yourself from your extraordinary potential, and the possibilities that time affords you. You have been gifted this time, so you can self-actualize. Self-actualizing your gifts will add joy into your journey. Sharing your gifts with others with the true essence of your being is where you need to invest your time. The gifts you have received in this lifetime are to be developed, and then shared with others. The universe will bow down to the one who has aligned themselves with their walk/purpose/mission.

As you check in today, count how many times you acknowledge or refer to time. You can speed time up by doing things you love, or slow time down by doing things you have to do. Regardless of how you spend your time, the days, years, and decades of your life march on. You neglected to appreciate your youth by wishing time would pass quicker, so you could reap the benefits of being older. You then discovered you yearned for the time when you were younger. We wish our days will pass at lightning speed so we can get to where we want to be, only to then wish time would slow down, and allow us to enjoy the things we want to last forever.

I encourage you to take the time to embrace the true essence of your inner being, appreciating the virtue of time and molding it into a beautiful space, so you may dwell in the spirit of love. Enjoy all the moments life offers you, not just some of them.

How quickly the years and decades pass, making it hard to remember exactly what we did with our time. Did we simply spend it? If we spent it without thought, it owes us nothing.

You might be saying to yourself that this is all well and good, but it is not your reality. I invite you to make a record of the activities you are involved with for one day. A record of one day provides you with a window to see what you are doing with your time. Our brains trick us into believing we are maximizing our efforts, and that there is no more room in a day, to complete your tasks, but this isn't true.

Grab a piece of paper, use a whiteboard, or develop an Excel spreadsheet, and make a chart of your whole day at fifteen-minute intervals (some things do not take longer than fifteen minutes). Record everything you do – for things like self-care and sleeping, consider blocking those hours to ensure that time is accounted. Include leisure time, like watching a movie and scrolling through social media to get caught up with your friends. This is not an exercise to have you remove things you enjoy from your day, but rather an opportunity for you to gain clear insight of the things you spend your time doing. Once you educate yourself on what you are doing, only then can you become the master of your time. Becoming the captain of your journey allows you to self-actualize your life.

When you can assess yourself accurately by this exercise, you change how you see what you are doing and what you are omitting from your day. Most of us do not have the conscious awareness to realize our shortcomings. If we spend time in thought, contemplation, and revelation, we allow ourselves to self-actualize, instead of running thoughtlessly after the next gadget, next promotion, next fix. When you align yourself with receiving gifts, instead of subscribing to the hamster wheel that has you chasing after success, you create a happier and more fulfilled life. This allows success to enter the field of your awareness.

You may cultivate your gifts from the essence of your being by looking inside yourself. Some may hold onto their current reality at all costs, even at the expense of personal health, until something deeply and profoundly impacts the way they understand themselves.

People have often asked me. "How do you have the time to do the things that you do?" I protect my time. I have things I need to do, and then I have things I want to do. I am awake in the early morning, so instead of trying to find sleep for another hour or so, I get up and begin the things that I enjoy; the activities and tasks that help me align with the truth of myself and my gifts. I create, meditate, drink coffee, and go on a long brisk walk, all before my business day begins. That gives me time to enjoy my personal routine that prepares me for my daily business tasks — the "must-do" things.

Take time and mold what you want to do, accomplish, and enjoy in your life. Take it and compartmentalize the things you want to do, and then allow some time to do just that. If you are spending your life not liking what you are doing with your time, you need to address that truth. You must spend time figuring out why you are here, and what you have come here to do. You do not want to spend the latter part of your life wishing and regretting anything. Everyone is different, and each person's journey is unique to them. You simply need to get in touch with what your journey is meant to be.

But we do not know the possible outcomes of our decisions, or do we? What about that part of us, those whispers that guide us, warn us that something good or bad is about to happen? We slough it off as we pay more attention to our egoic self, that part of us that we chat with occasionally.

We must subscribe to time to make a living, to raise our children, and we cannot forget about time, because if we do, we are left behind. Our children are evaluated by the doctors for size and assessed by a chart. They are either on, behind, or ahead of where they need to be at that moment in their life and development. If you are not ready for a certain category of sports, or for a certain grade, you could develop an attitude which causes you to arrive to that moment later than what was expected of you. When you hear others refer to you as average, you may live out a so-called average life. You may subscribe to a reality that you only need to put so much into life because you are, "what they said," average. Embracing this mindset suppresses your talents and causes you surrender over your true potential. Many, however, have risen above their conditioned selves and succeeded despite the labels they were given.

Some have fallen into a rhythm of a lifetime of working for one company until retirement. People talk about retiring at 60, so they can do the things they have held off doing. They are "doing time" to get more time to do the things they love to do, want to do, have been waiting to do – remembering with each tick of the clock that time is marching on. Many people have heart attacks and die as soon as retirement comes. Why retire anyway? Why not continue to live your life to the fullest, no matter what stage of life you are in?

Time is attached to our hearts and our health; it keeps us from dying — sometimes. It brings us joy and laughter or pain and suffering. Those who were late did not die during the bombing of 9/11, the sinking of the Titanic or the many plane crashes. Their lifelines were not interrupted, their lineages exist today because they were late. They were too late for work, too late to board the ship, and too late to catch that plane where people perished. They survived.

People whose blood pressure soared because they were late and were short with those they loved, fell victim to the power that time held on them and their existence. Time of death is recorded. And yet, for the rest of us, time marches on.

***

To contact Rhonda:

rhondagrantauthor@gmail.com

www.rhondagrantauthor.com

Amazon.com: Magical Forces Within: Extraordinary Discoveries in an Ordinary Life (9781525577031): Grant, Rhonda: Books

Podcast: The Rhonda Grant Show – C-Suite Radio (c-suitenetwork.com)

LinkedIn: https://www.linkedin.com/in/rhonda-grant-57586584/

Facebook: (2) Rhonda Grant Author, Radio Talk Show and Podcast Host | Facebook

Instagram: https://www.instagram.com/rhondagrantauthor/

Arline Warwick

Arline Warwick is an international speaker, author, founder and owner of Find Corporate Sponsors, LLC. She shows businesses, entrepreneurs and nonprofits how to find hefty sums of money, "Money you don't have to pay back" that can be used to build your business or organization. Arline has spoken on several panels including the United Nations Parallel event and has presented on many stages with internationally known speakers and New York Times best-selling authors such as David Fagan, Suzanne Evans, Larry Winget and Dannella Burnett.

Years of working with animals, babies, special needs children and adults has made Arline a strong, proficient, and intuitive connector of people, businesses and non-profits.

She teaches you how to build your base, partner with local businesses and corporations then work your way up to the national corporate sponsorship level. After learning from her own experiences and years of research, Arline shows you how to guide your business through a step-by-step system that reveals the easiest approach to finding the best partnerships so you can grow, blossom and bloom. You don't have to be big to get sponsors, sponsors make you big.

Your Connections Determine How Much Money You Make

By Arline Warwick

How would you like to make money while helping others?

Would you like to have your name and pictures on national corporations' websites and in their newsletters?

And...would you like to receive hefty sums of money to build your business? This is unlike a business loan. This is money you don't have to give back.

All of this is possible when you partner with corporations and have them sponsor you and your business. Don't get confused between donations and sponsorships. Donations are gifts. They are monetary or in-kind gifts given to charities and nonprofits. Sponsorships, on the other hand, are partnerships where are you create a symbiotic relationship with each other. When a company sponsors you, your business or nonprofit works together with your sponsor. You give them more exposure, visibility, credibility, customers and clients, and return on their investments. By working with sponsors, *you* also get more exposure, visibility, credibility, and more clients or customers.

A client of mine made a 900% increase on her investment within 2 1/2 weeks of reaching out to sponsors. Want to know how she did it? Are you open to exploring ways that this would be possible for you? In a moment I'm going to share with you how you can do this too because I believe it's time for you to go full force and make a great difference for yourself, your community and the world. Would you be interested in finding out how helping others could help you build your business? Of course, you would!

I believe that even the smallest contribution can make a great difference in the world.

And...I believe we have the ability to make this difference but have been sitting back too long, not taking charge of our full potential because we simply don't know where to begin.

I'm sure you are driven but you just don't know where to turn or how to start. You have tried many things, but nothing seems to get you to a higher level. Is it a constant struggle sometimes? The bills keep stacking up, you don't have time for your family, you're over worked and the phone doesn't stop ringing.

I can relate to that feeling

I was in my kitchen one morning when the phone rang. It was my niece, Kimberly. She said, "Arline, I don't know what to do you've got to get here right away. I just don't know what to do". I could hear the distress in her voice. We rescue feral cats, and she found a group of cats at an old fish camp. I rushed down to meet her and when I stepped out of my car I was horrified. I stepped into a sea of cats. There were little kittens with feather weight bodies. They had heads as big and round and dense as golf balls. They could barely hold their heads up because they were so malnourished. I started picking them up and putting them into my pockets and stuffing them down my shirt! I didn't know what else to do. That was the changing point. It was like someone slapped me in the face and showed me reality. Right then, I knew I had to make a change. I had to do it immediately. We didn't have the time, energy, manpower or money to take care of that many cats. That moment changed everything for me. I was driven.

It took years of research and trial and error learning to find a solution. I finally got it! I realized that our connections determine how much money we make. I also realized that "You don't have to be big to get sponsors, sponsors make you big". So, if you are struggling…Get a corporation to sponsor you. The money is there, but you're not finding it because you don't know where to look. In 2018 corporations gave away over $60 billion to businesses and nonprofits. So few know it's available. Why would a big company want to sponsor you, your business, your organization? You might think you're not well known, you're new, you don't know what you have to offer. Is it possible you might be belittling yourself, not realizing that corporations need you? Companies need you so they can get in front of new audiences, attract new customers, make direct connections with your target audience, grow their customer base, drive sales, the list goes on and on. With the right tools and strategies, you will become an asset to them. You're never too small, you're never too new, and you don't have to be a nonprofit to work with a corporation. Let's take action! Do you feel you are here to accomplish incredibly important things? Do you feel deep down inside that if you had the right strategy and a blueprint you could make a huge difference in this world?

You know you can do this. How quickly are you going to make it happen? Always remember this: you don't have to be well known to get a sponsor. Sponsors make you known.

Would you like to know how to begin? First, you need to build a sturdy base, a beginning blueprint. To do this you must start locally. Even if you have an online business, it's pertinent to become known locally. Come up with a simple project (you do not have to put on an event). Just start a project in which you can involve the community and your sponsors, a project where are you are helping those in need. What you want to do is make your sponsors community leaders and local heroes. When this happens, free press is easily attained. Free press and advertising is available from your local radio stations, from your local newspapers and TV stations. Local magazines will write articles about you and spread the news about your "Give Back" project. Think about it. Let's choose a car dealership as an example. A car dealer will spend tens of thousands of dollars for an ad on TV. But that's all it is... An advertisement. They say things like, "Come in we have slashed our prices, we have the best financing in town." The list goes on and on. They are missing something very important and crucial to having people pay attention to them and respect them. They are not giving back to the community, and this is where you come in. This is your chance to give them more exposure, visibility, credibility and make them local champions. You then become a champion right along with them.

Would you like to establish a partnership with your sponsors in which you are both "Doing Good"? Remember, you do not want to ask for a donation or for help. Your desire is to help them gain more recognition which will help them with their marketing goals. According to Mashable, "90% of Americans are more likely to trust and stay loyal to companies that actively try to make a difference. 88% of consumers say they would buy a product/service with a social or environmental benefit and 84% would tell friends and family about a company's corporate social responsibility (CSR)". Your objective is to build a long-term relationship with your partner/sponsor. A relationship in which these corporations will sponsor you year after year. That is the goal. And the great thing is, you can have as many sponsors as you want.

This is important...I cannot stress this enough...Do not ask for a donation, do not ask for help. You are offering them a chance for more visibility and credibility. Please do not forget that ever. Please make sure you realize it's all about what you can do for them, your sponsors. It's not about how great your business is, what great products you have and how much your nonprofit has done. It's about what you can offer them, your potential partners. Many of the local companies that will work with you are franchises. They are branch offices of national and international corporations. Car dealers, restaurants, daycare centers, hardware stores and assisted living facilities are just a few examples.

Now here is the real secret!

Corporations want to look good. They want and need new and refreshing content. The competition is great for corporations. They need new ideas and projects. They want positive energy coming their way. They need original and positive information to post on their websites, in their emails and in their newsletters. By building a local foundation and working with local sponsors you create beneficial content. You have current and constructive information. You have pictures and videos and articles about what their branch offices have accomplished in your part of the nation or world. Corporations want to personalize their companies, their products and their services. Wouldn't it be great to help them do this? Wouldn't it be great to become part of their team? You now have the perfect segue to reach out to them and communicate with them. You have information, valuable, up to the minute information for them!

Sponsorships are not industry specific

What does that mean? When you want to become known locally (remember this is where your recognition and credibility begin) it's important to involve as much of the community as possible. You might think that because you're a health coach your potential sponsors must be in the category of health food or exercise. Or if you are a realtor, you may think you must have sponsors that fit into the category of finance or building materials. When you are involved in a local project the entire community is elemental and each of the businesses in that community would be potential sponsors for you. Do you think it would be beneficial to be able to drive traffic to a local restaurant that is your sponsor or to a motorcycle dealer that is your sponsor or a furniture store, etc.? What it comes down to is the entire community is a great match for you and your project.

When reaching out to sponsors be bold and ask for what you want. You are providing value to their company. You are helping the company market itself. You will not get what you want unless you ask for it. Again, start locally, build your base, generate and assemble great content, build a relationship with companies and franchises in your community. Compile your information and content so you are not reaching out to corporations cold. Make the "Big Connection" with fortune 500 companies by showing them what you have produced and how valuable it is to them. The goal is to go huge! Reach out to, connect and collaborate with national and international corporations by starting small and working your way up. Building a base gives you tremendous opportunities to work with higher level businesses. Corporations are not going to come to you! You have to go to them. If you are consistent and persistent the money will follow. What it boils down to is this: Are you ready for a second income? Do you have the desire to go after it? What is the next generation of your business going to look like? Are you ready to try something different? Do you want the benefits of obtaining extra money and security? Are you going to

take the steps to create new possibilities for yourself and your company?

This is how she did it:

Earlier, I mentioned a client that made a 900% return on her investment within 2 1/2 weeks of reaching out to potential sponsors.

Tina lives in Winston Salem, North Carolina. She wanted to do something for the medical Covid workers in her community. She decided to collect items (with the help of the community) to assemble into gift bags which she called stress relief bags. She reached out to businesses in her local community to see if they would be interested in sponsoring her for putting on the project. She had a marketing plan for them which drove traffic to their businesses. She also was able to get vast amounts of free press for them since they were involved in a community project. She spotlighted the businesses as being leaders and superstars in the community. Within 2 1/2 weeks of reaching out to these local sponsors she received a 900% return on her investment. This was money that she was able to use to build her business. She could use it on anything she wanted such as travel expenses, hiring an assistant, purchasing a new computer, anyway she saw fit. The money did not go to the medical Covid workers. The collection of items went to them.

This was a four-way win!

Tina won because she received money from sponsors that she could use to grow her business.

The sponsors won because they became known in their community by being the "Good Guys" and being spotlighted as heroes. They also had more people coming to and visiting their places of business.

The members of the community won because they had the satisfaction of being able to support the Covid workers.

The medical Covid workers won because they received gift bags and felt appreciated for their hard work and devotion.

Now Tina is working with the corporate levels of these franchises (community businesses) to attain her higher-level goals to fulfill her dreams. Tina took action. After working with local businesses, she had valuable information and content. Using this material is the perfect segue to reach out to the upper-level companies.

Do you believe it's possible for you to take the same kind of action as Tina so you can fulfill your goals and dreams?

Do you believe it's possible that people who help each other can have a four-way win situation?

Do you believe with the right strategy and tools you can have an extra income when partnering with corporations, an income that will help you become known nationally and internationally while receiving funds to build your business empire?

Be bold and ask for what you want. You are providing value. You are helping companies market themselves. You won't get what you want unless you ask for it. The great thing about partnering with corporations is the sky's the limit! You can build a relationship with your sponsors so that they will sponsor you year after year.

Do you think it may be possible that your connections determine how much money you make? Is it time for you to connect? You can be a tipping point for corporations. Competition is tough. To stay on top of the game these industries must always be looking and implementing new ideas. You can play an important part by giving them exposure. Show these companies how you can help. You can create more customer loyalty for them, reinforce their image, make people aware of their new products and services and show your audience that corporations have a social responsibility known as cause related marketing.

Do you think it's possible that if you had an eye-catching proposal and a plan of action that you would appear attractive to potential sponsors, and they would want to work with you?

Remember, it's all about *them*…your sponsors.

Think about what you can do for *them*. Let *them* know how you can give *them* more exposure to bring in more customers.

Communities are looking for leaders to emerge. Take this chance to become a strong leader. You, along with the community and your sponsors, are the ones that will make mini miracles happen! It's time for you to flourish. With a vision, project and the right guidance, you will find it's easy to work up a plan of action to "Do Good" in your neighborhood.

Once you have gained the knowledge of the interworking of sponsorships you will be confident enough and feel powerful enough to connect with corporate icons, work with these icons and create with these icons. Connections make all the difference in the world and these connections will determine your growth and success. I'm sure you don't you want to stay where you are if you are struggling and feeling defeated. Maybe you're not exactly struggling but your business has just plateaued. Do you feel you have reached your peak and you have not made the progress you would like to make? Here's your chance to barge ahead and try something new, different, fun and exciting. Something that can bring enormous amounts of success. Do you want a greater sense of security? Would you like to become an expert in your field? Would you like to make money while helping others? Would you like to be seen as big? This is all possible for you. Just reach out to my calendar link below so we can set up a time to talk and you will be surprised how capable you are of getting top notch sponsorships.

Whatever your business, you can accomplish great prosperity and celebrity through sponsorships. You can work and partner with the icons of the world. Don't be sidelined by the fact that you don't have enough experience. Get out there and do it. You are sponsorship worthy!

"Change your life today, don't gamble on the future, act now, without delay"

~~ Abraham Lincoln

16th US president

***

To contact Arline:

Arline Warwick 386-212-6892

calendar link: www.getsponsorshere.com/schedule

www.Findcorporatesponsors.com

info@findcorporatesponsors.com

Janelle Cameron

Born in Brisbane, Australia in 1961. I am genuinely flawed! I'm also grateful for all of my unique experiences that have led me to be able to accept myself today as a totally awesome human being. In fact, it is the flaws that allow me to be in this position to inspire and support so many to become who they were meant to be…in every area of life!

My family of origin didn't get the memo about, *The Times They Are A-Changing* and certainly not about the increased acceptance of *Sex, Drugs, and Rock N' Roll*. Hence, I was trying to straddle two worlds. I entered my adulthood full of fear and without a useful set of values and strategies for success.

The results of this part of my life caused great pain and suffering. One way this played out was my attraction to anything that would numb my emotional pain. I had the conditions for the perfect storm to tear through my life in the form of alcohol and other addictions. Short words here can't explain the horror of that part of my life. I had it all, a beautiful house in the suburbs with a husband and two beautiful children. However, I came very close to losing it all.

Fortunately for me, while at high school, I stumbled on to a learning strategy that worked for me. I've always been a successful learner, teacher and leader (1985 - 2020 Education Queensland).

It was in fact a colleague's words that cracked through my denial. That moment gave me the courage to utilize a way of life that has allowed me to go from Despair to Daring to Live my Dream!

Challenge Culture with Compassion

By Janelle Cameron

My colleague's words cracked through the denial of the reality I had built to protect myself. This occurred as a result of me saying, "You could tell she had a liquid lunch today". He swiftly said in his best Canadian accent, "Janelle, that's what people say about you." My delusion was shattered in that moment. I sought help for my drinking problem within a week.

The first step towards the prosperous life I have built began in that moment. I was shattered because I thought I was doing a great job of keeping my drinking a secret. I learnt from an early age about how to protect myself. One strategy I had been unknowingly using was to avoid disclosing my feelings, thoughts, and actions. Why did I not feel safe to openly share parts of myself and how and why did these self-protective, yet destructive behaviours start? I can look for clues in my upbringing. In fact, all my adult life up until the age of thirty-nine, I blamed my family and the life we lived controlled by the "regulations" handed down through the doctrines of the Salvation Army. Some facts related to my upbringing, did contribute to my state of fear and sense of being overwhelmed. Instead of drawing a line in the sand and acknowledging my family for doing the best they could with the tools they had at the time, I drank alcohol to bury the pain. I needed to have taken 100% responsibility for how my adult life could be. So, the amount of alcohol I drank fed my victim story and further warped my thinking. This dysfunctional pattern of thinking and behaviour continued for many years.

Once I started taking 100% responsibility for my thinking and therefore my behaviour and actions, I went from victim to victory. I have experienced deep forgiveness for myself and all of my imperfect parts. I am able to connect with the reality of my life by concentrating on what is in front of me and being mindful and laser focused; one thing at a time. Cracking through the denial was the first step to the "rich" life I have today. I started telling my secrets and began to have compassion for myself. I was then able to take the second step to changing my life. This involved changing the narrative. The story I told myself had to change as I awakened to the actual reality of my life. Once sober though I felt that I needed to keep my sobriety a secret. This was not caused by propensity to keep secrets. It was the stigma of being recognised as an alcoholic. There is still a stigma attached to being an alcoholic, whether you are two days or twenty years sober. Today my mission includes breaking down the dominant culture's ideology about people with active addictions and those in recovery. My aim is to work with business and community leaders to highlight how to create spaces where people in and recovering from addiction can be compassionately understood and supported to recover.

On the cusp of the global pandemic, I was diagnosed with breast cancer. As lockdowns began, I visited the hospital daily for treatment. I had been retired from my thirty-five-year career with Education Queensland. I had been searching for my 'next' when I was originally diagnosed. I did not have the sense of urgency that I have post cancer. I am eternally grateful that I found The Coaching Institute. (Remi Sharon Pearson's Founder and owner, Melbourne Australia). As a student I have access to world class teaching, modelling and researched and scientifically proven models to apply firstly to my own life and then to help others. My next was born, Nextthought. One such model is The Critical Alignment Model. It has four parts. I am following this model and am 100% clear about the legacy I am building. I am gaining a platform to spread my message. My values, attitudes and beliefs are again aligned, and I can create structures to effectively implement these systems. It is a replicable system, so I can teach others to either do this in their own life or business from scratch or fill in the gaps to be more effective. This model and my own teaching experience and IMPACT framework, combine to assist me to shine an even brighter light on awareness of mental health and its importance to the health of our global community. My story is not unique; however, it does prove that it is possible to recover. With support from many beautiful and patient people I have been able to go from 'Despair to Daring to Live my Dreams'.

The Critical Alignment Model insists that we are clear about our mission first and foremost. How many of us learnt this during the formative years? As an adult, I needed to develop my own Mission in life, my own values and beliefs and standards as they were at best confused. For example, one of my first memories is begging other kids to play school with me. I always had to be the teacher. In Brisbane in the early 60s there was black and white television and only a few programmes on one of three channels. This was my only 'worldly' source of ideas. My other source was Sunday school and church. Some people have fond memories and ideas about the Salvation Army helping and supporting people. While this is factual it is often not known as a 'religion'. It was founded by William Booth in London in a response to the poverty and misery caused by the industrial revolution. Its structure is developed along military lines and there are regulations. My father was a 3rd generation soldier in this army. It formed my parent's identity and gave a set of rules to live their lives by. It was an upbringing that did not encourage me to be a healthy confident independently free thinker. For example, being a girl, I had to stand in front of the band and play the timbrel, a tambourine. I did not have a rhythmic bone in my body and was temperamentally extremely unsuited to playing in this way. When all of the other girls finished with their timbrel down by their side, mine would be up in the air or vice versa! You get the picture. Also, imagine my horror when the decision was made to build a new church on a vacant block right in the middle of where many of my fellow classmates lived. To survive, I convinced myself I was invisible to these kids. Of course, I wasn't. My state school experience was brutal. I desperately wanted to fit in. At a twenty-year reunion, my fears were confirmed when a fellow classmate made a bee line for me and told how he and his friends used to hang out of his bedroom window and laugh at me dressed in my soldier's uniform which included a hat! By the time of that reunion, I was in the last throws of my active alcoholism. To this day I have no knowledge about how I arrived home.

I know I did not have a healthy thinking pattern and I am still not clear why I told the first lie. I do know that secrets were necessary for my daily survival, for me to feel safe. Like the way at eight years of age I lied about being sick and stayed away from school for three months. The reason for this lie is still very vivid in my mind. I could not face the "fail" mark on my maths sheet. I could not manage to ask for the sheet to be signed by my parents, so I pretended to be sick. This evolved into guilt and then paranoia. That pattern of paranoia about people finding out about my truth has taken me to some dark places. Lies permeated my life. They became entrenched and habitual. It was years later in my early years of sobriety that I finally found that I could forgive myself and was released from the burden of guilt and shame.

The second and third parts of the Critical Alignment Model include Structures and Implementation. It is possible to create thinking that pushes us to the edge of our comfort zone where all positive outcomes are possible. The person who is 'stuck' in addiction or any unresourceful thinking does not have these set up in their life. People are the fourth part of the model. By reflecting on all my relationships, I was looking to be rescued. This caused me to be vulnerable to being groomed during my teenage years. People are at the core of every successful outcome. By ensuring that the culture is set with aligned systems and processes focus can be on people. It is within workplaces and communities that rich relationships and connections that are healthy can identify and assist people if they need help to get back on track in their thinking. It is widely reported that the use of substances and alcohol has risen during the pandemic. Therefore, this awareness and action is everyone's business.

A particularly difficult part of my journey from 'Despair' has been to confront the reality of some decisions I made in my life. I am not responsible for such behaviours from my childhood. I was a kid trying to survive. It becomes less clear cut when I reflect on my teenage years. An example of this is an experience I had with a Salvation Army Officer my father sent me to for Career advice. There was a drug and alcohol rehabilitation centre associated with our corp. (Church) The Salvation Army Officer groomed me from the time I was fourteen to seventeen to have a sexual relationship with him. As an adult I reported this to the police and put in a complaint that was investigated. No financial compensation was awarded as I was older than the age of consent. Again, I slipped into blame and shame. This relationship in my formative years did impact my life in many negative ways. Part of the healing process was to change the narrative I told myself. I needed to take myself out of victim mode by having compassion for that adolescent girl who felt she had nowhere to go and no one with whom to share the story. I have learnt that secrets have the potential to kill. My drinking story is typical of any practising alcoholic woman. My first drink was at a school party, and I remember coming to, out of a blackout as I was walking home. I had no idea blackouts were not normal as I always experienced them. As anyone who has experienced a blackout is aware of the horror of not knowing what has happened. To wake up in the correct place is such a huge relief. This is followed by the habitual checking for evidence of the missing hours.

Another way I have found to not regret the past is to tell my story honestly and share how I have healed. It is inexplicable to me now, that at the age of twenty-six I had an abortion as I

was unable to tell my family I was pregnant. At the time this decision and action exacerbated my debilitating fear of confronting my truth. The most difficult part has been to forgive myself. I am a product of the environment in which I grew up. The power of my family, because of the indoctrination of the Salvation Army, was real. The only way I have been able to be reconciled with the decision to have an abortion has been through a spiritual path. To find forgiveness I needed to find connection with something outside of myself. I needed to open my mind to spiritual possibilities in contrast to religious doctrines that I had rejected for many years. As hard as I had desperately tried to make a connection with God from an early age, I felt nothing. Sunday night I would be full of fervour to do God's will in exchange for help through my days at school. I had searched for a magical source outside of myself to rescue me from reality. Today, I have a connection with the source of universal love deep within myself.

Confronting my reality required a great deal of support for which I am extremely grateful. I have accessed professional and community services and support from people who showed up at the right time with the exact message I needed. These invisible threads to my recovery are still present today. I started to build trust in myself. I became the person I was always meant to be. The greatest paradox of all is the knowledge that as a little 7-year- old child I pledged to God to never drink alcohol and within nine years I was a practising alcoholic. Subsequently I did go to hell on earth. Today, I know that it was not me breaking that promise that caused this trip to hell. I have learned to have compassion for that seven-year-old and understand how my journey can help others 'Dare to Live their Dreams' as well. I'm so grateful I got to crack the rich code.

I have shared the HOW of my sobriety with many women and have so much gratitude for the life I have built over the last twenty years. I have found the greatest peace in the connections that I have learned to build with people. Even though I surrendered to not being able to manage my drinking and that was the defining moment of my life; it was not enough. I had to find a way to drive past the bottle shop on the way home. I love sharing the HOW this happened. I needed to start to meet my core needs and overcome the three universal fears. Philosophers, psychologists and sociologists, discuss how we must have our physical needs, including safety, met before we can advance to other needs on a hierarchy. Practising addicts and alcoholics have precarious access to meeting this core need. There are many who would say of my story that you had all of your physical needs met and that it is your own fault that you drank. You were delusional and do not deserve to be loved or included and you certainly do not deserve to belong. In fact, you are a fraud! These are all comments thrown at me. They are well known the three universal fears. It is hard enough to claw our way back from the pit of despair without this type of real commentary. Destructive self-talk is hard enough to overcome. It is only by having the first faltering days of recovery that these turn into weeks, months and years that turn into decades. This experience informs my work and my mission.

To minimize the devastation an active addict and alcoholic causes in society it is imperative that we change our attitudes and develop compassionate hearts. It is my philosophy that substance and alcohol addiction is a disease. By the time physical dependence has occurred it is a medical problem that requires medical intervention. The use of the drug is a symptom of deeper emotional problems that need to be healed. It is also I mental problem. The brain's function is severely impaired by lack of nutrients and limited unresourceful thinking patterns. The work in neuroplasticity informs this work as well. There are many freely available programmes for addicts and alcoholics. My work does replace or interfere with those. My mission is to change the stigma attached to addiction and alcoholism.

I also am calling on leaders in our communities to hear that I was successful in my career and yet I am an alcoholic. I had to continue my lifelong habit of keeping secrets in order to be recognised as a true professional, unencumbered by the stigma attached to alcoholism. It is still judged by many as caused by weakness and lack of morals and good standing. I stand against shaming and ostracising addicts and alcoholics, using or recovering. I am a voice against the dominant culture that condones use of alcohol but does not take personal responsibility for its links to injury and death. Maybe I had to crack the code for myself!

As Australian schools embarked on the Digital Revolution, I travelled throughout Australia delivering a workshop that was part of an online and face to face training to assist teachers with integrating digital pedagogy into their classrooms. It was during this time that I developed a digital framework. After many years of developing effective teaching and learning strategies and utilising my knowledge of learning theories, I constructed a framework that was later widely developed and used by Education Queensland. It is the IMPACT framework that I now use as the methodology in my coaching, mentoring and tutoring work. It starts with to Inspire. My story From Despair to Daring to Live my Dreams is an inspiration to anyone who wants to overcome obstacles in their life. This includes anyone stuck in their own victim story who is having trouble moving forward. To inspire someone to trust in themselves enough to do the work to transform their own life is an amazing gift and privilege. New learning or thinking requires Modelling across all learning styles. For effective teaching and learning to occur the person's preferred or dominant learning style needs to be identified then utilised. I also believe that the person modelling excellence needs to be authentic. They need to have travelled the journey and thereby have compassion for the person undergoing the transformational work. This new way of being must be supported in a non-judgemental environment. With success, their confidence will grow. By Practising proactivity instead of reactivity, the person will build competencies and confidence. This in turn provides an opportunity to incorporate the new thinking into their lives. There needs to be an awareness and acknowledgement that while willing to change this new learning is being incorporated into sometimes a chaotic life. There is such a need for people to have a supportive network outside of this coaching relationship. For example, when I became sober, I knew I was trying to learn to change my self-talk and live responsibly. My life though, had been built on fear and my victim narrative. To consciously change this way of thinking required laser focus. When applying this new way of thinking and behaving to their life, they need to be supported. My e-learning background enables me to support people from all over the world via Zoom. For example, from a classroom in Brisbane I have taught students on yachts in the same class as a student in the back seat of their family's car travelling around Australia. Other students have been sitting under gum trees on their family's remote property or perhaps they are sick in a hospital trying to have a normal part of their life in school. To Communicate this learning in a new context is essential. To Transfer the learning into all parts of their life is a challenging time. They are often working out for the first time who they can truly trust. All of the 'people pleasing', and co-dependent behaviours are decreasing. I use a variety of questioning techniques to help people realise they are not using resourceful ways of thinking to change their own lives.

Transformation and personal empowerment are becoming a new reality. To witness this transformation is such a gift.

I am also inspiring business owners and leaders to use The Critical Alignment Model to check the culture at their workplace. By fully utilising The Critical Alignment Model's four parts I can assist people to find their own mission in life. Employers can check if they are providing a safe work environment for all people. Employers have a great opportunity to **impact** the acceptance that society, in general, has on alcohol. It is insidious and destructive and goes against so much of the great advancements we are making towards mental health. It is a fact that drugs and alcohol can lead to personal and societal destruction. I believe it is every individual's responsibility to check if they are consciously working towards promoting a resourcefully rich environment that is inclusive of addicts and alcoholics, using or recovered. It is my privilege to be working in this space of cracking the code on this destruction. I trust you will join me.

***

To contact Janelle:

https://www.facebook.com/janelle.cameron.77

http://linkedin.com/in/janelle-cameron-7b515595

www.nextthought.com

Pamela Monasch David, MBA

Pamela's mission is to empower people to reinvent their lives and businesses. A business is reflective of the core energy of one's self. She specializes in the transition from employee mindset to that of an entrepreneur.

The majority of her professional career was spent with the Macy*s corporation in the cosmetic and fragrance industry. Having reached a senior level management position, she transitioned into the world of entrepreneurship beginning in media (Radio) and the point-of-sale industries. She founded a Special Events company serving the SF Bay Area and Sacramento, CA markets for innumerable Corporate and Private Events.

Pamela is dedicated to empowering and transforming businesses and individuals. She has served her community as a Board Member for The River City Theatre Company (RCTC), as an Ambassador for the Sacramento Metro Chamber of Commerce and various other community organizations.

Today Pamela is the Best-Selling author of

The Reinvented Life book and is Co-Founder of KissEla Agency Business Advisors.

She is a fifth-generation San Franciscan, and holds a BS in Speech and Auditory Sciences from *University of California at Santa Barbara* and Masters of Business Administration (MBA) from *Drexel University* in Philadelphia, PA. Pamela is the proud mom of three adult children and resides in Sacramento, CA.

Celery Salt Isn't Just for Hot Dogs

By Pamela Monasch David, MBA

Imagine sitting in the stands at Chicago's famed Wrigley Field. The summer day at the ballpark is beautiful and the crowds are cheering an exuberant roar. The Cubs just put another home run on the board. While unwrapping the hotdog you just purchased from the vendor climbing up the stairs, you cannot help but get an immediate whiff of the celery salt. There are things in life that just seem to "go together." What's a peanut butter sandwich without the jelly? Or a beach in Cabo San Lucas without all of the sun umbrellas? The Chicago Dog, seasoned with celery salt, is just one of those trusty pairs.

But what about other uses for this special seasoning? For most people, a jar of celery salt will sit unopened in a dark recess of a cabinet or on a spice rack and rarely get used. People forget it is great in salad dressings, a Bloody Mary or a compliment to many other everyday dishes. Forgetting about alternative uses or new perspectives is analogous to what happens in life. People tend to get their minds made up about a particular use of something or an idea, and then that is it. It is this singular way of thinking about anything in life or business that can be limiting, even destructive. The way that something "has always been done" can stifle progress. Moving away from this thought process is key. It is the definition of flexibility. When one is more innovative and flexible in thought, it can be powerful. Even one's emotional state can be uplifted and improve when one releases the notion that there is only one way to be. Options, in life, provide openings. Openings subsequently create space for greater potential and growth. Thus, growth and greater flexibility form the framework of reimagining and reinventing.

Embracing Transitions

It was not until I was in the position of urgently needing to reclaim my health (which had spiraled out-of-control) that I recognized the need to increase my flexibility. After years of ignoring my physical body, obesity was staring at me as I looked in the mirror. Somehow, I had managed to avoid paying attention to it. I ignored the dangerous impact of not taking care of myself was having. I now had to face the struggle that comes from such a deteriorating health state. I had to wake up to how I was running my life. Truth be told, how my life was actually running me.

Flexibility was a key tool for me. I had to recognize that the conditioned thoughts I had known weren't going to support me to transition from almost losing my life to living a healthier one. I had to move my body in ways that were unfamiliar. After all, I had subconscious programs running that I was not athletic. Thus, to infuse fitness into my life, I had to start with creating new thoughts. Mentally, putting new thoughts in place about what I was capable of allowed me to emerge healthier. The struggle to lose over 150 lbs was real. The need for physical changes in my life paled in comparison to the mental and emotional transitions I needed to make. I had to move out of a state of denial. When I had previously needed a seatbelt extender to buckle up on an airplane, I had simply blown it off and thought that it was no big deal. I hadn't been facing reality. I knew I needed to embrace change. Prioritizing my own power and how I could better serve ME was all new. After all, my life up until that point had been caring about everyone and everything else. Yet, infusing new ways of thinking and how to reinvent has now become the basis of my life's work. I can now embrace the principles and lessons I have learned to inspire countless others in a myriad of ways.

Times are Messy

The global pandemic has affected every family, organization, industry and community in one way or another. Lives have been lost. Plans interrupted. Some have embraced new opportunities throughout, and some have retreated. Life has been put on hold for some. It continues to feel messy. People have been isolated, distanced and are operating with uncertainty like never before. We are facing new, painful challenges. It has shifted expectations in life and business.

Global shifts in the economy are finding individuals, in unprecedented numbers, moving from corporate careers to entrepreneurial endeavors. Corporations themselves have faced huge shifts in the way they are addressing business. Everything from the landscape of how work is conducted to where work is done from is up for evaluation. In fact, relevancy of every aspect of life is under evaluation. The shifts in purchasing habits have caused innumerable changes. This new landscape has left organizations and companies to face layoffs, closures and restructures. The silver lining is that new efficiencies and more receptiveness to change have emerged.

There has been a drastic exodus from the corporate ideology to one of entrepreneurship. Many individuals are thinking about career and earnings in a new way. There is often times a new awareness that takes place in this shift to one's emotional, physical, intellectual and even spiritual state. In other words, how one has operated before may no longer serve them sufficiently. New ways of thinking are required.

Change: Get Prepared

Change, in any form, requires flexibility and grit. Using the example of moving from a corporate environment to one of entrepreneurship, there are new roads to be traveled. This is true in other transitions as well, relationships, community work or even within families. When transitioning into anything new, the first phase generally is associated with feelings of freedom and independence. This new-found independence can be exhilarating. It can also seem foreign. New paradigms and conditions will require different thought processes. New habits will need to be formed. In the example of a corporate transition to one's own business/entrepreneurial endeavors, things will arise that previously were not of concern.

As an entrepreneur, insecurities may emerge to the forefront and cloud the clarity of your judgement causing conflict to arise. Things that previously seemed "right" may now seem "off," or even wrong. The key is to embrace this process as you are naturally adapting to a new way of life. To crack the rich code in your life and business, you must be willing to adopt new patterns of thought and correlative actions. Taking leadership in your own life is what will determine how rich we are; rich financially, how healthy, rich in relationships and in our communities.

Manifesting abundance in all of these areas is where the grit enters the equation. Adaptation and evolution take work. One of the greatest life hacks is to do away with the notion of failure. There are only two states of being, that of success or that of learning. Everything we do may not result in the exact, desired outcome. However, the fortitude to take those learnings and keep moving ahead will be essential for growth. Momentum in a forward direction will keep one's business and life full.

The Strength of the Inner Game

Business is a reflection of our core inner self; our mental and emotional being. Therefore, what is happening on the inside is more important than what is happening on the outside. This outer game is the projects, the "achievements" and the tasks. What we are doing. How often have you felt as if you were "working as hard as possible" on something, but were not getting the results you were aiming for?

Likely, *quite often.*

The probability is high that energetically what (or how) you were working on is likely out of alignment with your spirit snd truth. Re-examining your thoughts and framework will become your best friend. As we evolve through life, it makes sense that we can't operate from the same vantage point since growth has taken place on our journey. Scripts that have driven our behavior over time naturally become outdated and out of alignment as we grow. It is only when we open ourselves energetically to new ways of being, that more endless possibilities unfold.

Reinventing can also be a return to our more natural self that has long been forgotten about or lost along the way. Traveling on our unique journeys of life can manifest the next steps we take. For many of us, we begin to run on autopilot. Our lives begin to take shape not necessarily incorporating intentional behavior but allowing ourselves to default to the next step. Ironically, we later spend energy and effort deconstructing why we are where we are. Strengthening one's inner game allows one to ignite or reignite passions and purpose. It is generally that moment in time when one starts to think more expansively.

When thriving, and not just surviving, we can hold space for grace to reimagine.

Eliminate Beliefs

A newer entrepreneur as an example, may have become conditioned through being an employee. He or she is likely to have adopted the notion that their value is determined by what they produce or achieve. The idea that "what you've come to believe" or "I am who I am" may in fact, be detrimental to growth. As counterintuitive as this may sound, starting the process of eliminating beliefs can prove most helpful. As an example, if you continually think that you're in a process of overcoming obstacles, you will continue to create obstacles. This is so because your inner thoughts/energy (often referred to as subconscious thoughts) are still focused on obstacles. Yet when beliefs go away, possibilities now arise or reopen up.

Beliefs are constantly formed throughout one's lifetime. Reevaluating those formed beliefs becomes especially important, and unfortunately, one of the most commonly overlooked things that people do. In fact, quite the opposite usually happens. We mix up beliefs with our ideals. We cement ourselves, wrap ourselves in and attach ourselves to these beliefs. Eventually, if we see the need to move away from those beliefs not serving us, it can feel as if we're abandoning ourselves and "who we are." The essence is that people can maintain valuable pieces of their character while dissolving certain beliefs.

This is the number one reason that human beings do not move forward. We forget about options. We get terrified of "what others may think." The familiar takes precedence over over what could be more favorable. Losing sight of this, and just staying in a comfortable place, can hinder expansion. We tend to forget other purposes. People simply don't remember that there are new and multiple uses for the celery salt.

Small Shifts can be Significant

Interestingly enough, one small shift in a thought, can lead to an entire new way of being and an igniting of new passions. When guiding and coaching clients to consider new business opportunities, life shifts and decisions, one common thread tends to emerge. Similar to the pull of gravity, falling back into old habits, thought patterns and ways of being happens frequently. With proper guidance, partnerships and collaborations, the thoughts and action to move forward can happen. Small shifts can create newness. Redefining progress can be liberating.

This new-found freedom allows us to step back from labeling ourselves as this, that or the other. It is discovering that limiting one's definition and construct of oneself will be a new beginning and often times, fresh or increased confidence. This can lead to converting comparisons of oneself and others, to curiosity of new exploration.

Using new entrepreneurs as an example, relief will come with the realization that they no longer need to be limited by the heights they can reach. Although it may feel scary (unfamiliar) in the beginning stages, generally speaking, they will be able to be more intentional about what they can now strive for. Wisdom and experiences can now be springboards they can launch a future off of. Being in a place of creation will eventually form the foundation of new thoughts, with new correlative actions and the formation of updated habits.

The newer habits can replace more limiting ones. Entrepreneurs tend to have a spirit about them that prioritizes wonderment and curiosity. Habits will develop into routines. Therefore, it's incredibly important to be sure the habits you develop are serving you and the direction you want to go. The starting point to this evaluation is training the mind (developing habits) to eliminate hesitation and doubt. Without this purging, there is a mixed signal sent to oneself. This condition can show up as over-analyzing causing huge stunts in growth. When we train our minds to show up with conviction and be decisive, we are helping ourselves get clear.

This habit of developing clarity will be one of the greatest tools you can develop for yourself. Use it liberally. Letting anyone obscure that clarity will prove detrimental to your growth, business or life plans. Fear is one of the significant emotions that drive the fading of clarity. Often times, fear rears its ugly head because a clear destination may not align with previous thought processes. It can feel scary. Channeling your thoughts towards where you want to be versus where you had previously been going will be vital. Thus, keeping the "what if's" alive in creating new possibilities will create cloudiness to your clearer vision.

Where to Begin

Start with gratitude. Whether you're at the top of your game, or desiring changes in your life or business, the same principles hold true. Gratitude is about being in action and more than just being thankful. Gratitude allows one to gain clarity and peace as to where they are. Remembering that we are holistic beings, gratitude should center around all facets is our lives. The richness of our gratitude affects our quality of life. It affects one's soul. It strengthens our being and connections in the world.

Focusing and collaborating with supportive others will enhance not only business results, but life results. An important phase of any business creation or project in life is who you are on the boat with. It is vital that even a "solopreneur" or an individual working on his/her own, collaborate with someone. Gathering supportive coaching, expertise or advice can prove invaluable. The right team surrounding you can actually elevate your productivity and the impact you can have on others. Being intentional and focusing on impact can energetically make a substantial difference in your success. It will increase confidence about knowing that what you are doing actually matters. This knowing that one individual can inspire another begins to shift productivity. The inner game is now driving results. This sheds light as to the importance of one's story and energy that is put forward. Today, relatability can accomplish more than technical skills or even talent. It can inspire others to begin their own new journey. Realizing that others can open up to new possibilities based on other shared experiences increases personal confidence and purpose.

Alignment, therefore. with "what makes us feel whole," will be reflective on the outside outcomes. Learning to trust something that is new can feel daunting. Yet growth is the most natural state to be in. When moving more effortlessly by flowing rather than operating with a fixed way of being, new opportunities will emerge.

To crack your own personal code, believe in endless possibilities, not outdated, misaligned notions. Be open, get flexible and most importantly remember:

"What you allow, and who you allow around your life's table, will determine the speed and extent of your reinvention."

~ *Pamela Monasch David, The Reinvented Life book*

***

To contact Pamela:

E: Ela@kisselaagency.com

P: 916.803.7461

https://kisselaagency.com/

https://www.thereinventedlife.com/

FB: https://www.facebook.com/pamela.m.david.9

IG: http://instagram.com/pamelachaneldavid

LI: https://www.linkedin.com/in/pamela-chanel-monasch-david-mba-6532ba2/?ltclid=

T: https://twitter.com/the_reinvented?lang=en&ltclid=5aa458d3-9c9d-443a-a620-ef50b169df47

Greg Herlean

 Greg Herlean has spent the last 15 years focused on growth opportunities and wealth accumulation through real estate vehicles. His aptitude for business has afforded him the opportunity to provide management direction, capital restructuring, investment research analysis, business projection analysis and capital acquisition services. He has personally managed over $1.1 billion in real estate transactions. He has flipped over 450 homes and 2,000 apartment units. He has also purchased and sold 12 hotels.

When he founded Horizon Trust, a New Mexico based custodial company, Greg took his mission of educating Americans on the power of self-directed accounts to new heights. At Horizon Trust, his experience and in-depth knowledge of SDIRA industry market dynamics are frequently leveraged and employed. Moreover, it allows Greg to educate and empower self-directed investors every day. Greg is also a sought-after platform speaker on the topics of estate planning, capital development and investment growth through use of self-directed IRA vehicles. These speaking engagements allow him to share his expertise with others who are interested in obtaining greater financial security.

If you really know Greg, he has all the tools to make calculated risks and he has become successful because he with almost every fiber of his being is an entrepreneur. He currently resides in Las Vegas, where he is an active member of the community.

Why Self-Direct Your Ira?

To Create a Lifestyle That Gives You Complete Freedom!

By Greg Herlean

"The question isn't at what age I want to retire; it's at what income."- George Foreman

I'm about to get in your face about money.

Why? Because I know you could be doing more to maximize your assets, to create greater income and build a better future for you and your family. I'm excited about helping you succeed because I've learned that financial success is simply a combination of attitude, aptitude, and action. This chapter is about changing your perspective to see all the tools you have at your disposable to change your financial future. It's about financial facts that most American's haven't yet been exposed to. It's about empowering you to take control of who is in charge of your money.

A self-directed IRA enables you to utilize your IRA to fund investments other than traditional mutual funds, stocks, or bonds without having to depend on a financial advisor. My goal is to help you bring your IRA out of passive retirement and begin maximizing your assets with a self-directed IRA. I'm going to share how the self-directed IRA's have allowed me to become the "bank" and to "live" life on my own terms.

When I was a kid, I was constantly hanging out at my friends' houses. I didn't truly understand why I would spend so much time at their homes until later. Of course, a home where there was fun, and love is ALWAYS important. But I also noticed I would spend time at friends' houses where the parents were home and doing fun things during the day with us kids. Even though my mom was almost always around, my dad was always working. I wondered why my dad always had to work, and other dads didn't. Later, in my childhood life, I would wonder why we couldn't have certain fun things like a boat and others did. I quickly decided to learn what other people did to create income to be home and do the things they wanted.

Retirement to me is just a word, not something I ever thought much about nor still think about—a lifestyle with my family and friends to do what I wanted, when I wanted became my goal at a young age. Everyone's why is different, for you, retirement might be when you can stop the daily grind, and that's fine too. But learning how to make money, how to make it work for you and to be with family more was my goal and what I got good at.

> "I've got all of the money I'll ever need if I die by four o'clock. - Henny Youngman

Self-Directed IRAs (SDIRA's) were the format that I learned to create my bank using my retirement account. A self-directed IRA is an IRS-approved vehicle established in the mid-'70s that allows individuals to make money without paying taxes on the gains. If you use an SDIRA with a ROTH account, then you could essentially not only have you're investing growing tax-free but also come out tax-free. Now that I have been in this industry for over 18 years, I find it interesting to hear that some traditional financial firms offer an SDIRA. Let me tell you now that it is NOT true. All established financial firms and brokerages can only share with you conventional market options in which they make money if it goes up or down.

A SDIRA is done through a licensed Trust company like mine, Horizon Trust Company, and others. Let me tell you though SDIRA investing is not for all people. It's for the people that can take the time and energy choosing investments they want to invest in. Approximately 70% of our clients use their SDIRA's in real estate. From investment rentals, notes, whole-selling, REITs, funds, etc., etc. The other 30% is comprised of people using their SDIRA funds in gold or precious metals, businesses, cryptocurrencies, or other things. It's exciting and life-changing at the same time. I don't want you to read that I say "life-changing" and not understand why. By understanding what an SDIRA can do and taking control of it, you can create a passive bank-like investment portfolio or any other portfolio you choose.

That is why I say that you need to take control of it - NOW. Growing up, I watched my dad work 60-80 hours a week. Although he worked hard to earn money, he never took the time to focus on his retirement planning. He depended on those advisors to watch out for him, just like many of you are doing right now. My mom was the only one who even looked at his 401(k) statements. She would receive my dad's quarterly statements, see if they went up or down, and then file them away, not ever knowing what the funds were invested in, nor understanding the fees they were paying.

The only time financial planning was even discussed in our home was when my dad would get a new advisor, who would call to make sure the account was intact, and his commissions were secure. I also noticed that my parents weren't aware of how much they were saving, and their financial advisor never called or looked in on them. So, they didn't have a plan for retirement or a team that would help them achieve their retirement goal.

Watching that is what made me keenly aware that they still didn't care as much as I did about my family's money, no matter how great the financial advisor was. To those financial advisors, my parents were a dependable annual commission, and a secure account. That's it, and that just wasn't enough for me.

That is why, as I learned more and more about self-directing, I helped my parents take control of their money, too. Once I learned how to successfully self-direct IRAs, I showed them how to take control of their retirement account. I have now taught tens of thousands of people this concept and am proud to say I have helped over 10 thousand people find and understand the SDIRA concept with our company at Horizon Trust.

Recently I flew to Palm Springs to be a guest speaker at a weekend financial seminar. I was due to speak on Saturday. I arrived Friday night, and the event had already started. During a break, there were people out in the foyer. I was standing around, catching bits of conversation here and there.

I overheard a young guy in his early thirties talking to a few women who were probably five years older than him. He said, "I don't think I'm going to go to the IRA presentation tomorrow because I'm too young for that. Why do I want to learn about money I can't even touch for 30 years?"

I made a point of seeking this gentleman out the next day and told him how I did my first real estate deal when I was in my twenties using IRA money. Soon, he had a whole different perspective and brought all those ladies to hear my speech, as well.

What he realized was that he didn't have to wait 30 years to retire. He had built that timeline in his head. The truth is you can retire when you have enough wealth to do it. For some, that may be 65. For others, that may be 35. Why wait if you don't have to?

It's another example of making a choice and doing what it takes to get yourself where you want to be. Having an IRA and knowing how to utilize it best will change your life! All you need to do is learn how to use the tool and go for it. This applies to everyone.

One of the biggest problems with young people today is that they don't even consider their retirement years. They aren't yet worried about it. Mainly because they don't want to be in a position where they think they have no control over their money. Again, this is just another fallacy. The truth is that now, more than ever before, young people need to pay attention to their retirement. The significant part is that the tools they need are right at their fingertips. Another belief that most Americans (of all ages) hold is that they do not control their retirement money. They accept that they can only select investments from the four choices that their employer or financial advisors present to them. They assume that they cannot use their retirement money to invest in real estate, make loans or fund a business. If they took a look at that belief, they would discover that they have complete control of their retirement money if they choose to take the reins.

I got into educating people about IRAs because it's a financial resource most people are passive about. Since the whole concept of retirement may seem like a long way away, they don't actively engage with this money. They think, "well, I can't even touch this until I'm 59 ½, so I'll just let it do whatever it's supposed to do, and X amount of years from now, it'll be enough for me to retire." The sad truth is that people spend more time planning their next vacation than they ever do on their retirement.

Then, around age 50, they begin looking at it and realize that it didn't perform as well as expected. But if they had known about all of the opportunities available to them, they would have been more excited about the possibilities and gotten more involved.

How many of you remember that first sit-down meeting with your advisor where you put together this hypothetical scenario that if your money did X and you put in Y amount of dollars for Z amount of years, you would be set for life? How's that working out? Just like your advisor said? I know it didn't because it never does.

Now, I know I have said that young people need to start planning for retirement. Some of you are probably asking yourself: "Well, I'm over 60. What about me?" So, let me address that now - of course, this pertains to you, as well.

For those over 60 years of age it's not too late to get started with a self-directed account. If anything, your time is even more valuable because you are already using your retirement money to live from. You want to get that money working hard for you as soon as possible.

I have a client, Anne, that came to my team at Horizon Trust. She wasn't pleased with her financial advisor when I met her and was looking for other options. She wasn't just upset that her portfolio was underperforming. She was also upset that he never called her, and he never made any attempt to make sure that she was getting everything that she could, she had $420,000 in her IRA, and she decided to dip her toe in the water on some real estate trust deeds.

I knew that Anne would be a little bit harder to win over from the moment I met her. She was skeptical, and she was already upset with an advisor that she didn't feel was genuinely looking after her. After two months, Anne believed she understood the concepts, so she took a little risk and invested $20,000, representing roughly 5% of her assets.

By lending $20,000 from her IRA, Anne was now the bank. She went into a real estate transaction (trust deed) that provided her security funds against a tangible hard asset. Soon, her IRA wasn't bleeding anymore because she got a 5-10% fixed return. The loan was paid off after nine months of interest payments and returned all the original capital.

Anne lends her funds on properties that are between a 50-70% LTV (loan-to-value) and, little by little, has come to understand how to vet deals and how the whole process works so that she can put her funds in a passive banking position. This is done primarily on her own and with other people that we're able to educate her. I've had others like Anne take control by buying cryptocurrencies and double or triple their money in one year using their IRA and pay no taxes on those gains.

Anne learned the concept of becoming the "bank" faster than others. Have you ever wondered why banks were closed on EVERY holiday and had the best hours for their employees? "Banker Hours"... It's because they figured out how to use their money and other people's money to work for them. Getting to a place where you can be the bank and working as a bank with your money is what I call the banking stage. This is where you graduate from active to passive investing. This is where you fund deals for other investors. This is where you free up your time and start to live the life you want on your terms. Remember earlier in the chapter I mentioned I learned to be the "bank" to "live" life on my own terms.

In this "bank" stage, you are growing your passive investment portfolio and beginning to remove yourself from the active tasks in your business. You are strategically placing your money into investments that will afford you a healthy lifestyle for years to come. This does not mean you need to take on more or additional risks. Yielding 5-12% per year on your money passively is all you need to do. It will take some time and work (like 1-2 hours a month), but the dividends you will yield with that time are priceless. Just think about the last time you spent 1-2 hours on your investments. I would bet that you have spent ten times looking or thinking or planning your next vacation spots in the last 3-6 months. It's just a fact. It shouldn't surprise you that most people are not prepared for retirement. Spend time (calendar it if you must) on your investment choices.

There is a country song with a lyric that says, *"there's a difference in living and living well"*. Living—living WELL—is both the end goal and the final stage is what I was told. That you have to wait until you retire in order to live well. BUT what I learned at an early age is to live well now – don't wait; time waits for no one.

You can live well but within your means while growing your bank and nest egg. Being the best human being, we can be to each other and ourselves is critical. The less time I have to spend stressing about money, the more time I have to enjoy my time with those I love doing the things I love. This is where all of your hard work and strategic planning pay off for you and your loved ones. The living stage is all about living the life you deserve and working when you want to—vacationing when you want to. Spending time with the charities and projects you care about. This is the stage where you are living your dream and giving back to your community.

Today hundreds of thousands of people like you are Self Directing their funds to avoid paying taxes and take control of their financial future. They are being the "bank" and creating the life they want to "live" on their own terms.

At Horizon Trust company, as a boutique licensed Trust company, we help individuals every day to take steps to prepare for their future but also their everyday lives. It's my mission to educate Americans about something that most won't ever hear about. It's my mission to encourage both old and young to invest in what they are passionate about. Like I said before, this concept is not for everyone, but if you're looking to invest in what you understand and know and not leave it 100% to people that don't typically have your best interest in mind, then it's time to Self-direct your IRA or start one now.

I often share the importance of just changing what you do a mere 2%. What does that mean exactly? I can tell you that if you adjust the way you look or the way you invest your retirement funds just a little (nothing major) and can earn an extra 2-4% per year on your funds, it's the difference of you having a few extra hundred thousand to a million in your account when you go to retire. What does that mean? That's the difference if you have an extra 2-10k a month coming in passively in your later years. I decided a long time ago that when I got my accounts, I would know exactly where all of my savings and investments were located and how they were performing; I would always be in control of my retirement money. I want you to take control of your money! Take advantage of an IRS-approved account! Start Self Directing some of your funds!

***

To contact Greg:

Horizon website: www.horizontrust.com

Horizon Facebook:
https://www.facebook.com/HorizonTrustCompany

Horizon Instagram: https://www.instagram.com/horizontrust/

T. Edith Gondwe

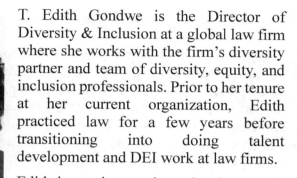

T. Edith Gondwe is the Director of Diversity & Inclusion at a global law firm where she works with the firm's diversity partner and team of diversity, equity, and inclusion professionals. Prior to her tenure at her current organization, Edith practiced law for a few years before transitioning into doing talent development and DEI work at law firms.

Edith is passionate about developing the next generation of leaders, particularly women and more specifically women of color. She is also focused on finding ways to define success outside of traditional models to create more space for diverse slate of professionals to thrive. Additionally, she supports leaders and managers to develop an inclusive lens when working and leading across differences.

Born in Abidjan, Cote d'Ivoire and raised in the Washington metro area, Edith has developed a love for studying how different people across the world live. That love developed through her international travels as young girl including family trips to Malawi, the country of heritage. In her travels, she has been particularly drawn to places like Brazil, South Africa, London and Paris because for their diversity.

Edith lives in Los Angeles and in her spare time enjoys global music, outdoor workouts and hikes and cooking.

Reimagine: Developing an Eye for Inclusion

By T. Edith Gondwe

The world is at a crossroads today. The Taliban take over in Afghanistan. Fires in Turkey, Algeria and Greece. The politicization of the pandemic. The lives lost during the pandemic. The fight for a unified front during the pandemic. 50,000 homeless citizens in Los Angeles (my home city). Rampant food insecurity. Racial discord and unrest. Intense and fatal weather patterns. The list, as we know, could go on for thousands of pages.

If we want to assign any responsibility to these events, we can only look to ourselves. We humans – humanity – have fueled the flames for what regularly feels like a chaotic, disconnected, disjointed, apathetic existence on the planet. More specifically, the thirst and quest for power – economic, social and political – is at the center of it all. These are present in every segment of society – individuals, corporations/organizations, governments, etc. Throughout the world, we have come to believe that there is only enough for a select group. The rest of us are left to fend for themselves. The rest of us are on the fringes, where it seems we are left to be satisfied with our status. Or we are left to fight to be a part of that select group or take what they have. Either way, we – the people – across the globe are polarized. And most of us, particularly in countries like the US, are just getting by, unhappy or convinced that this all life has to offer.

But do things have to be this way? Is this how we are supposed to life? Or most of us relegated to a life of apathy, misery, or mundane lives with some sunny moments? Are we destined for lives where connection, universal joy, cohesion and community are absent?

These are questions that I have been asking myself in the last few years. You see, I am one of the ones on the fringes. I am black. I am a woman. I'm in the 99%. And in the United States, my family are recent immigrants. For most of my life, I have been clawing my way to be in the select group. Clawing to have some share of the power and be happy. The American dream taught me I could have a piece of that. We all could as long as you work hard. Things, however, are not that simple.

Yes, I worked hard and achieved some success by most people's standards. I went to law school, practiced law for a short while and I lead a team at a global company. But I ask myself, would things be different if I were white? Most of the women of color in my life would emphatically say yes. Don't get me wrong, white women have incredible obstacles to overcome. I believe in a global sisterhood, but the fact remains that I probably would have had more promotions, greater compensation and greater access to all society's offerings if I were white. If I were a white man, the world of opportunities is vast.

To be blunt, if you are not a wealthy, white, straight male living without a disability, there are barriers to opportunities. Barriers that, at times, feel ironclad. Privilege lies in having few or no barriers.

And barriers to what? The American dream – a house, 2.5 kids in the suburbs, the foundation of freedom and power? In the United States, we all are taught to aspire to that but many of us never achieve or believe that. From where I sit, we should remove these barriers to thriving and living a happy life – however you define happiness.

Imagine a world where we are unified, connected and happy. Where community is at the core of society instead of economic and political power.

This may feel impossible but there are things that we can do. I know because of my own story. A story of a person on fringes who has learned about the power of inclusion – the power of diversity. A person who has seen that these forces – inclusion and diversity – can lead us to reimagining being human in this world.

THE LONE BLACK GIRL

I was born in Cote d'Ivoire, a country in the western part of Africa. French was the first language I spoke. My parents are from Malawi, a country in the southern part of Africa. My father was working in Cote d'Ivoire at the time of my birth. My middle brother was born 16 months afterwards. When I was 3 years old, my father's work contract ended and we moved to Washington DC. For my parents, a return to their homeland after a few years in West Africa was always their plan. Instead, they had my youngest brother a year after our arrival in Washington. When we left Abidjan, Malawi was ruled by the dictator, Kamuza Banda and it was too dangerous for my parents to reestablish themselves in Malawi. Thanks to the Banda regime, my brothers and I were raised in the US during the 1980s and 1990s, a time where few Africans migrated to the country.

From age 4 to 14, I was the only black person in my class. There were roughly 35 to 40 students in my grade in each of those eleven years. My school was a small, private school outside of Washington DC during the early to mid-1980s. The suburb I grew up in was affluent and very white. We had some international presence in town, since DC, being the nation's capital, is a hub for foreign embassies, international organizations and multi-national corporations. My family belonged to the international organizations segment of the DC population, since my father worked for the International Monetary Fund/World Bank. Belonging to this community was a lifeline for my family. Because of the presence of this international community in my suburban town and throughout DC, people in our neighborhood seemed open and kind for the most part. While the people in my suburban town were still predominately white and mostly affluent. And my family was black and middle class.

Like any young child, I tried hard to fit in with the rich, white kids. It was not easy. I actually remember a few moments of my first day in kindergarten. I recall walking up to a group of kids who were playing together in the classroom. I had tried to start a conversation. They responded. Both they and I had confused looks. I couldn't understand their English. They could not understand my French. From that moment, I felt like no one would be able to understand me, so I would have to work hard to understand and be one of them.

My kindergarten career was the start of my journey of assimilation in my grade school years. I learned English (and had to relearn French later). I adopted a "white" accent, which I still have today. I wore braid extensions often because my hair would "look" long. I wanted my fellow students, friends and teachers to forget that I was black. And certainly, I wanted them to forget that I was African. And while this approach seems to work for me, it still always caught up.

When I was roughly 9 years old, I heard my first n-word joke. A group of us were walking together to our next class, while one of us told a joke where the punch line was the "n-word". Of course, he and the others in the group were white. I was stunned. Thankfully, my other classmates were also stunned, and they immediately stepped in. They told him that he was wrong for telling us the joke. They warned him to never repeat it. He was taken aback. It was only a joke, he said as he looked me in the eye, seeming to beg for my validation. After all, if I was one of them, why wouldn't I laugh at the "n-word" joke? And from what I remember, he never shared another racist joke in my presence again. He had learned to ignore that I was black and African and by doing so did not really "see" me. I was reminded that I was the only one who looked like me.

It was one thing for my classmates to make feel like an outsider, but it was quite another for my teachers to do so. When I was 13, during Black History Month that year, 7 of my white teachers sat be down in a room and asked me how it felt to be black. All eyes and smiles were on me. I told them that I don't know.

While I could not put my finger on why that instance with my teachers bothered me, I knew it was irresponsible of the teachers to put me in that position. Up until that point, I had allowed my classmates and teachers to give me nicknames because they could not pronounce Tiwonge, my first name. I had made sure that I was always smiling and happy, so people could see that I was approachable and friendly. I had befriended the rich, popular white girls in the grade. I thought I was one of them. That I belonged but sometimes, I felt like a novelty, an outsider. Was there really space for me to be me? The experience with my teachers made doubt this.

WRESTLING WITH MY IDENTITY

For most of my childhood years, I wanted to be white. I wanted to be skinny. I wanted to be blond. That is the image I saw of beauty, grace, admiration and inspiration in the media, all around my town and most of all, at school. During the 1980s and 1990s, my childhood years, the mainstream was white and seemed to have no room for black women with the exception of shows like "The Cosby Show" and "Different World." Most of the black shows, magazines, music, etc. in my predominately suburb white world were considered fringe culture. At school, I would play along and loved what classmates loved. At home, it was a bit of a different story. At home, I was exposed to elements of black America through my mom's younger brother, who was raised with us like an older brother. He came to live with us at age 14 and had close white friends at school. Outside of school, he was part of a small group of Malawian teenage boys who lived throughout the Washington metro area but mainly in places where there was actually a critical mass of black people. Through him, I learned to love black American culture, particularly rap music, R&B, break dancing, etc. I loved everything he loved. Looking back, what he exposed me to made me feel like I had a sense of belonging.

Throughout my childhood, my parents also reminded us that home is always Malawi. Malawi was the land of our people and ancestors. They would regularly share stories of their upbringing, play African music legends like the late and great Miriam Makeba and Hugh Masekela. We ate Malawian food at home every day. What was particularly valuable for my brothers and me was our family trips to Malawi. Through my father's job, we were afforded the opportunity for home leave back to Malawi every other summer. On those trips, I spent time with my beloved grandparents, aunties, uncles, cousins, etc. I was welcomed with open arms. They taught to me where we came from. I felt and still feel proud to be of Malawian heritage.

But still I struggled to reconcile the pride I had in being Malawian and black with the insecurity that I had with being the only black person or one of few. That struggle was most evident during my college years. I went to a progressive and diverse liberal arts college in New England, where I learned so much in and out of the classroom. While during high school I finally had 5 other black people in my class (one of whom is still a close friend to this day), I did not feel a deep presence of black people on campus until my college years. Having a deeper presence of black people at school sparked a new insecurity in me: was I black enough? All of the black and Latinx students, who mostly came from the NYC Burroughs, seemed to get along. They also all seemed to have a quiet confidence that I lacked. I held back when I would hang out with any big groups of black and/or Latinx students because I sounded "white". I was also insecure about my family being African immigrants (as opposed to black people whose ancestors were enslaved). As a result, I found myself heading down a path of militancy and resentment towards white people. It took a conversation with my mom when I returned home from school one summer to remind me that I was brought up to love and connect with all types of people. That conversation snapped me back into opening myself to all types of people. I made a conscious decision after that talk with my mother to more fully embrace my heritage and be open to having different types of people in my life.

When I graduated from college and began law school back in Washington DC, I immersed myself into the growing Malawian community in the city as well as forging strong connections with a cross section of law students, particularly other women of color. As a result, I became more confident in my identity and people seem to embrace what felt like the real me. The me that I had struggled to reveal to the world.

TAKING A STAND FOR THE MARGINALIZED

As I began my career in the legal arena, I gradually came to see that most people around me had homogenous networks, whether they were black, white, Asian, Latinx, etc. Global law firms, the institutions that I had belonged to for nearly twenty years, are particularly white, straight and male. From the beginning of my law firm career, I have had to hide or cover much of my identity at work. Doing so, I thought (and as many diverse professionals think), would open up opportunities for advancement, connections with colleagues and to strengthen my reputation. I made sure that productivity and always saying "yes" that I could have a successful career. But as most professionals of color know, eventually you'll stand alone or be singled out. That was certainly the case for me at various points of my career.

I remember the time I was called into my boss's office while working at a prestigious, boutique law firm in the Los Angeles office a few years ago. My boss, who also was my friend, had called me into her office because someone had complained about how I dress. Essentially someone complained that my clothing was too tight or revealing. I was stunned and disturbed. I never wore anything tight or short or too revealing. After lots of tears were shed in her office,

I went home to gather some advice from my mother and few of my close friends. All separately had said I was singled out because I was the only black woman at the firm in management (and one of handful at the firm) and I what people would describe as thick. It had not occurred to me because of the shock. I knew they were right but who at work, could I share this with? My boss was a white woman and would not understand. I felt frustrated and alone. From that time, I vowed that I would make sure that no other professional women of color I worked with would experience what I experienced that day.

During my tenure at the same law firm, Trump was elected President of the United States. For me, that was a difficult time because I felt that the diversity of the nation was under attack. I come to see diversity as this nation's greatest strength. I had witnessed the power of diversity in my own life even though I struggled with my identity growing up. Knowing and forging friendships with a variety of people through my life has opened up the world to me. During the Trump era, marginalization and hate became a tool to target groups traditionally marginalized in the US. Mainstream in the US equals a white, Christian and straight man's lens. Why does it have to be this way? I believed and still believe it does not. It was during this time in my life that I decided to dedicate my life to diversity, equity and inclusion. I then quit my job and never looked back.

REIMAGINING

Today, I lead a team comprised of women of color who are responsible for diversity, equity and inclusion at a global law firm. I work to ensure my teammates feel empowered to have an impact at our organization and beyond, particularly during this pandemic era and historic period of racial unrest. I aim to encourage them to be themselves at work and to interact with different people. We are passionate about making an impact and supporting our colleagues across organization by humanizing the experience of working in the corporate arena. We are focused on showing all of our colleagues, including our white, straight male colleagues that building equity and balancing the power at our organization and throughout society is good for all. Through my work, it is clear that we – our organization, the legal and corporate arena and society as whole –

need a new paradigm. We need to embrace our differences and live in such a way that everyone can feel free to be their best selves. We can reimagine what it means how we live. We can reimagine what means to be human, just as I learned to reimagine my reality as a black woman in America.

***

To contact Edith:

tgondwe@gmail.com

Dr. Andrea Adams-Miller

Dr. Andrea Adams-Miller, The Dream Maker, is an International Award-Winning Author, International Publicist, Business Consultant, & Sponsorship Acquisitionist who manifests your dreams bigger than you ever dared to dream possible. Just imagine how your life is positively affected when your right message, services, and products are known to the world.

A whirlwind of energy, she has shared the stage with outstanding leaders like Anthony Hopkins, Jack Canfield, Stedman Graham, Les Brown, Brian Tracy, and more. She has the authority, credibility, & connections to put you in the limelight, create JV's, set up partnerships & acquire funding. She holds two PhDs and Certification as a Master Neurolinguistic Practitioner, Master Hypnotherapist, Biofeedback Practitioner, and Neurofeedback Practitioner. Also, she has certification in about a dozen other healing modalities.

Additionally, as the Executive Director for The Keep Smiling Movement, a 501(3)c dental and mental health organization, she helps people discover resilience to handle any challenge put before them as the organization 'Creates a DOSE of HOPE through SMILES. She lives on a 50 acre Ohio farm with her husband, Tom. She is mom to three adult daughters, Destiny, Devony, & Demiya, and she loves being Glamma to Mavis, 5, and Warren, 2. For your free gift, the #LivingRED Publicity Challenge, visit www.TheREDCarpetConnection.com/FreeGifts.

Relationship Capital:

The Most Valuable Asset to Cracking the Rich Code

By Dr. Andrea Adams-Miller

Laying the foundation for wealth, defining what brings the value of money is disputed. Which of these words represents the value of money? Authenticity, honesty, rank, social class, intelligence, notoriety, stardom, fame, and athleticism. While these factors are assets towards wealth, there is something far more significant. The most satisfaction and happiness people have high-level relationship capital. The wealthiest are those that consider relationship capital the greatest asset. This asset is not taught in schools and is overlooked in society.

Before mentioning more about relationship capital, a more significant value is defining rich. Richness varies in meaning as I have met many a rich man alone, aloof, and unapproachable. In their sad state, they may be rich, but woe is their life where they have little connection with others to share. There are rich people with friends who tolerate their lack of social skills for items of luxury. The receipt of gifts causes them to overlook bad behavior. So these men and women, while prosperous, are the poorest people of all.

At the same time, many rich men and women live very happy, productive lives. They celebrate philanthropic adventures, authentic relationships, genuine connection, and true bliss. What is it that they have that the wealthy miser does not? What defines rich as a healthy, wealthy experience?

For you, the true goal is the desire to experience the depth of richness. The richness that comes from financial wealth is tied to healthy relationship capital. This richness is the wealth of connections, support, partners, friends, and family. True connectedness equates to relationship capital.

There is a specific framework for developing relationship capital. When the foundation is poured, it brings a solid landing that possesses a world of true happiness. This framework of being is often natural but can be learned. Relationship capital involves creating energy around you, having high genuine energy results in people's desire to be in your presence. It is the act of behaving so that people want to serve you and support you with your endeavors. Consistency is showing up as an honest person. That person is one with whom others wish continued deeper connection.

Your foundation is based on how you show up in the world. You show up with your presence, your who, and your why. It encompasses what other people see, feel, and hear. It is what people want to know more about you and your knowledge. In cracking the rich code, take this foundation beyond the feel-good, beyond the basics. Why? Building a foundation for true success means building a foundation for which you can stand firm.

You may wonder what happens if you don't build a more prominent foundation than you aspire to be. These entrepreneurs, business owners, athletes, and artists end up back at the beginning. They are forced to regroup to rebuild their foundation. They are forced back to the basics. They must build a stronger foundation to grow bigger, stronger, faster, harder, and more room to grow.

So how do you build this foundation so that it starts with a more solid footing? In my experience, it begins with personal development. Look back at the people for whom you most admire? Chances are, they took a deeper look within themselves. They now must take responsibility for what is and is not working and why and why not.

In investing in yourself about personal development, assess the following attributes. Do you have

· Knowledge – are you well-read

· Education – do you take training, classes, and certifications

· Wisdom – do you practice making decisions with educated risk?

· Self-awareness – do you address your fears and release your limiting beliefs?

· Share – do you engage in masterminds, network, go to events, and attend meetings

· Step out of yourself – do you take on untrained roles and responsibilities?

· Culturally Sound – have you traveled, gone to museums, learned a language?

Deep diving into these areas, reading is one of the most valuable gifts you can give yourself. But, in response to the reading suggestion, some people instantly push against it. They state they don't have time, don't like to read, and so forth. This resistance leads to a more poignant part of your foundation. For the future of richness, you must own 'YES' mentality.

The 'YES' mentality is one of the most important skills learned. I learned it from the theater, especially with comedy. For comedy to work, the other actors have a YES identity. A YES identity is the state of saying yes without objections and saying yes, knowing that you will figure it out. Say yes, knowing that there will be modifications, changes, addendums, and more ideas. When put into play, YES works for you. Thus, I ask you to put yourself into a yes mode when people make suggestions to you.

Saying yes doesn't mean you will or will not adopt the idea or conduct the activity. It means that yes, you hear the statement or question, and yes, that is an idea or possible answer. Then, consider the suggestions. Change it to fit your abilities, values, and principles.

Again, let's address reading. Maybe you are not a reader. Yet, you could listen to an audiobook. You could ask someone who has read the book for the cliff notes. You could download the Blinkist app that highlights the most poignant parts of the book. Additionally, find movies or documentaries that address the subject of the book.

There are so many adaptations to reading that allow you to read without reading the book. Thus, I hope for your sake that you can take this learning about reading and apply it to all areas of your life. Say yes, then figure it out. You can do almost anything you desire if you are creative and open to processing it.

Of course, reading coincides with education. Yet, education is not always defined as academic learning. Academic learning exposes you to learning outside your scope of understanding. It opens your mind to other possibilities.

At the same time, education does not have to be academic to be profitable and poignant—the information gained from informal learning on YouTube videos works.

The beginning framework seems simple enough that I refer to it as the ABCs of wealth. Authority, believability, and credibility are the three most important factors earned. This fact has proved true as I have discovered, learned, and taught others. So, let us continue to build that out, starting with Authority.

Your Authority is in Your Assets

Going through your past to note your accomplishments is what I call unearthing the gold. This info is the foundation of relationship capital. It gives you confidence so that when you speak, you know what you know. What that means is that you have this plethora of information inside of your head. I want you to think of yourself kind of like a library card catalog. When I was a child, we researched information in the library by searching the card catalog. These wooden cabinets were full of these little drawers. Each drawer contained hundreds of cards which listed a book title or subject label. These cards cross-referenced other similar or related information.

Your brain is like that card catalog. You pull out a file; let's say a file on academics. You will recall a class or training you took and remember something related to it. All the information on your accomplishments and achievements is in there. Nonetheless, you must dig for the deeper meaning of it. The reason is that you likely take all that information for granted. Your conscience didn't know that someday, we would want you to recall more than general info for a resume. You may have filed it away as insignificant or unimportant. You might think everyone has that knowledge.

However, that is not true. What you know is likely more than many other people know. So, to serve others with your wisdom and knowledge, you must stand confident in your expertise. You may not be the most outstanding expert in the world. Still, you are an expert, comparatively, to what other people may know about what you know.

The challenge proves your authority is for you to write down all your assets. Consider it a curriculum vitae but go deeper and broader. Write down everything you have ever attended, write down every meeting you have been on or participated in before. Did you watch a webinar? Write it down. Because that is one more reflection that is super important to what you're doing and how you show up in the world, that is part of your learning; write down the books you read and the people you know.

This exhaustive list is never-ending. As this document evolves are you evolve, so write, write, write, write, and write some more. Put it all down, separate it into categories, and start collecting that information. As you start speaking or selling your product, this information becomes valuable. As you open your business or sharing your services, this information becomes invaluable. Someday, this reference information will set you up for a great connection, a connection for a client to lock in an agreement. Or this list will lock in an invitation to do something more significant than you ever guessed. All these assets are the actual gold that you're unearthing.

Again, it is who are you. It is what you have deep inside. This document involves the following:

- writing down everywhere you've been
- everybody you know
- Finding photos you have with celebrities and business peers
- conversations you have had
- mentoring you have done
- topics that you have presented on
- classes that you've taken
- certifications that you had
- jobs that you held

Brain-dump it on paper. Transfer it to the computer. Then categorize it. Figure out everything about it. Recall the title, the timing, the time invested into it, where, who was there, and the value of the learning.

Make it a living document online. Every time you think or do something new, it goes on the list. Trust me. This document will be of extraordinary value to your personal and professional life. Asset recovery is a valuable tool for relationship capital.

Boost Your Believability

You become believable when other people say things about you. This social proof supports the relationship capital. It is an opportunity to look at your message, the soundbites that other people say about you. It is how you share yourself so that you show up in service of others. New businesspeople need to gather testimonials and reviews from their family and friends. s If you have been doing this a long time, revisit your peers. You likely never asked for a book review. Chances are you didn't request a LinkedIn recommendation. You probably didn't ask or didn't follow up on receiving a testimonial on video or a letter of reference. It's time to ask.

Along those lines, there is a believability factor of who you are in the world. So, when writing your bio, include the things others say about you. Using myself as an example, I share that my clients named me the 'Dream Maker.' Why? I care about their dreams, making their dreams come true bigger than they could have ever hoped to desire. That statement says something about what they think of me.

Additionally, they share that I was the recipient of the "Heart of Gold" award. I was nominated by 450 of my peers as the most giving selfless business professional. This honor is huge in meaning to me as it reflects what I desire to show the world. When people say things like that about you, live into them. Wear them like a badge of honor.

Credibility Abounds

Now that you have pulled all the videos and photos, it is time to share them. Credibility comes from social proof. You do that by putting logos on your website and your LinkedIn profile banner. You mention the accolades in your bio and your business description. Look at how valuable it is to say, "As seen on, 20/20, CNN, TIME, WebMD, CBS, NBC, FOX, PBS. Yes, that simple motion reflects the credibility that you have behind you. For that reason, I use those logos on my pages and state them in my paperwork and bios.

Additionally, list all the speakers for which you have shared the stage. At first, they may be interesting people but not well known. But, over time, these other people start to become more well-known. Some of them might just be the up-and-coming game-changers that you desire to know or be. For example, I have spoken on the same stage with many a celebrity now. These celebrities include Sir Anthony Hopkins, Def Leppard, Stedman Graham, Jason Alexander, Les Brown, Brian Tracy, Sean Callagy, Kris Krohn, Kevin Harrington, Jim Britt, etc. The privilege to share the stage with great people generates a level of credibility. This credibility increases higher than you can imagine over time and experience.

Keep going. List all the locations you have spoken at and the businesses. For example, as an international speaker, I've spoken all over the world. I spoke in Dubai, Egypt, Paris, Berne, Frankfurt, Belize, Costa Rica, Mexico, etc. The businesses for which I spoke include Sony, Google, the National Association of Broadcasters, and more. In your document, add the cities, states, and countries in which you spoke. Then add the businesses, colleges, and associations for which you have spoken.

Then add the fine details like the numbers of people who have heard you speak. For example, if you spoke on 100 podcasts with 100 listens to each, you have reached 100,00. These add up. Take, for instance, that I have been on over 2500 different radio shows. Add to that that I executive produce on-air a radio show weekly. This radio show alone has had over 2.5 million listens. My total outreach surpasses 20 million based on a lifetime of speaking and radio gigs. Hopefully, you hear the credibility in those numbers that align with relationship capital.

Always Remember the Power of Your Smile

As the executive director for The Keep Smiling Movement, smiles mean everything. We are a 501(c)3, a mental and dental health organization. Our mission is that 'We 'Save Lives with SMILES by Creating a DOSE of HOPE.' Frankly, we are HOPE Dealers. To reflect our mission, we use many acronyms:

SMILES stands for a Society Merging International Leaders and Entrepreneurs for Social Responsibility.

DOSE stands for Dopamine, Oxytocin, Serotonin, and Endorphins, HOPE stands for 'Hold on, Pain Ends.'

We thrive on relationship capital. Relationship capital helps others smile by creating a community of people. These people amplify goodness. They generate this outcome with their products, books, and services. All nonprofits, businesses, organizations, philanthropic endeavors, and more gain from our efforts. We amplify them through our books and referral services. To help people have the resilience to come out of the dark space, we share stories and have referral sources.

The nonprofit publishes your stories in short, condensed stories of HOPE. These stories show that there is a light called HOPE. You can find information to take part. Visit the Keep Smiling Movement website at www.TheKeepSmilingMovement.com. We offer this gift to leave your legacy as we want everyone's story to be heard. We are establishing that everyone is someone. We dream that everyone leaves a legacy behind. We want your legacy to be a source of inspiration, motivation, and hope. These stories generate HOPE for resilience for everyone else to thrive.

This gift is given because we want to lift, motivate, and inspire. These stories show resilience so that the readers receive that DOSE of HOPE. As a bonus, we build relationship capital. By establishing that you care about other people, you share your story. By contributing your story, you show love for others. As a result, the authority, believability, and credibility are increased. It increases by you being published by a notable source. It increases by being published alongside other people with significant significance. Our authors include influencers, celebrities, and movers and shakers. Authors are included like Ron Klein, the inventor of the magnetic credit card; William Paul Young, the author of 'The Shack,' now a best-selling movie; the Founder of Business Network International (BNI), Dr. Irvin Misner; the Founder of the Make-A-Wish Foundation, Frank Shankwitz; and Rob Angel, the Founder of Pictionary. As another bonus, you show 3rd party endorsement to readers as we must believe in you if we publish your story!

Often people don't realize the value of such an opportunity. Because they don't know how to use the gift to promote who they are, what they do, and how to change the world. Yet, being published with the Keep Smiling Movement, you share the nonprofit's mission. At the end of your story, we invite you to add your products and services are shared. You gain relationship capital by sharing the books as an eBook at the bottom of your emails. You gain relationship capital by sharing people or pages on social media. You gain relationship capital by talking about your experiences. You gain relationship capital by interviewing the other authors. Hence, you have content to share to establish the A, B, Cs of relationship capital.

Recapping What You have to Offer the World

In these examples, hear how you can share with relevance, enthusiasm, and delivery. These three words equate to what I call 'Living RED.' Look within your values and principles for your personal and professional life. Decide how do you want to show up so that people LIKE, KNOW, and TRUST you.

You hold power to change the world for the better. Consider how you want to show up with authority, credibility, trust. Shift that decision to include influence, social responsibility, social capital, and connection. Incorporating these examples, it is my purpose to make your dreams come true. I want to reflect that you have what it takes to show up in social media and traditional media. Your future holds radio, television, podcasts, stages, magazines, blogs, books, and newspapers.

This desire I have for you is based on unconditional love. I want you to focus on the ultimate relationship capital connection. If you have what it takes to show up powerfully in your industry, then all you must do is follow the steps above. By strengthening your authority, believability, and credibility, you build your relationship capital. You identify and elevate yourself from others. In finding that sweet spot, you will find yourself cracking the rich code. Then, you can prosper with wealth, abundance, and happiness.

***

To contact Andrea:

Dr. Andrea Adams-Miller

www.TheREDCarpetConnection.com

To book her for a radio show, podcast, blog, or stage, contact her at

AndreaAdamsMiller@TheREDCarpetConnection.com   419-722-6931

http://www.facebook.com/theredcarpetconnectionpublishingpublicity

http://www.linkedin.com/in/andreaadamsmiller

http://instagram/andreaadamsmiller

Rich Kozak

Rich Kozak is rocket fuel for people who want their Brand to *IMPACT* others' lives, or the world.

Rich is the sage voice of *IMPACT DRIVEN BRANDING*.

A four-time published author, Rich's next book, *IMPACT DRIVEN BRANDING — 7 Steps to Ensure YOUR Brand Impacts People's Lives, and the World*, shares the process in HOW-TO content, just like Rich shares in his online *Bootcamp* and the 1-Day Intensive Workshop, *"The Brand YOU Will Become."*

Rich, the **Founder & CEO of *RichBrands and IMPACT DRIVEN Publishing*** brings 44 years of experience Defining & Launching Brands, then Marketing them. He became a Certified Global Branding Consultant with partners worldwide, and Rich has defined brands *and their language* for companies and individuals across industries.

Rich was elected to the American Marketing Association International's Board of Directors; he took a "radical sabbatical" from his high-intensity career to reshape his life, to serve as chef to his wife of 44 years at his Southern California "Brand Ranch", and to earn new certifications as a master trainer.

Today, Rich also serves clients writing and publishing books that move their Brand forward. Rich's insight mentors you on steps to ensure your Brand really Impacts people's lives, and the world.

Rich builds and guides powerful brand platforms that *accelerate people into business success and into their purpose.*

What Makes Your Impact Driven Brand Come Alive and Attract the People You Most Care About?

By Rich Kozak,

CEO, RichBrands & IMPACT DRIVEN Publishing

Today, if you are an individual determined to make positive *impacts* on people's lives through your work, your business, your gift or calling, then you are a good candidate for the process of *IMPACT DRIVEN BRANDING*. It creates a foundation for your business that speeds your growth and success, then takes your impacts to a higher level.

Women and men who want their business to impact people's lives have a huge opportunity to use *IMPACT DRIVEN BRANDING* to stand out and attract. Often entrepreneur Brands lack the *clarity* they need in their vision and language. *Clarity* is needed to ensure *alignment* in all the Brand says and does.

Following the Steps of the *IMPACT DRIVEN BRANDING* process creates *clarity* and delivers *alignment* through powerful language and messaging.

Developing and launching an *IMPACT DRIVEN BRANDING* is important work, and we are deeply passionate about its powerful affects:

> your business thrives;
>
> you create a business platform that enables you to step into your purpose;
>
> you fulfill your calling;
>
> people whose lives you touch are blessed with high value impacts!

My name is Rich Kozak and I am the founder and CEO of *RichBrands*.

I am a certified global branding consultant who teaches the branding process, coaches individuals, guides companies, leads brand teams, writes about many aspects of branding, publishes books, for over 44 years, and today I speak regularly to audiences who care about growing *IMPACT DRIVEN BRANDs.*

I want my writing here to give you a gift and to accomplish four objectives:

1. Increase your awareness of *IMPACT DRIVEN BRANDING;*
2. Determine if you and your work are a candidate, and first steps you can take;
3. Give you an inside look so you know -- it's just a process, and you can do it.
4. Offer you resources and support to make the process easier for you.

Branding Distorted:

Unfortunately, the world has distorted people's perception of "Branding".

Many people aren't comfortable with the idea of "Branding" themselves or their company. "Branding" intimidates people. Some avoid even championing their own brand.

The Straight Talk: Branding is a Process.

I have invested over four decades defining, languaging & launching Brands, and I can say to you, with great confidence:

Branding is a process.

You do *not* need a *branding guru* to use the process.

You <u>do</u> need the process and a passion for your work.

You <u>do</u> need clarity of how your work will impact people.

By following the process, you develop a Brand that is *unique and authentic to you.*

The process ensures your Brand gets *credit for what makes you outstanding.*

The process develops a Brand whose *positioning is unique and defensible.*

These are all qualities of a well-defined & languaged Brand ready to powerfully attract its best target customers.

IMPACT DRIVEN BRANDING: Guarantees your impacts?

The process to develop an *IMPACT DRIVEN BRAND* has Seven Steps.

Each Step answers the question, "What does this Step require *in order to make the impacts we clearly envision* on people whom we really want to help?"

The Brand you define using the *IMPACT DRIVEN BRANDING* process is *The Brand You Must Become* to make the impacts you clearly envision. If you believe that sounds trick, I assure you it means exactly what it says. As a result, the process *guarantees* that you make your impacts. You make them sooner. You get known for exactly what you must be known for to accelerate your impacts.

The "hidden beauty" of the process:

Accelerating the impacts that your heart envisions making on people's lives also speeds you into your purpose. Caring to touch people's lives with specific impacts is an act of love, so God's hand is in it, believe it or not. Others "on your team" want those impacts made on more people's lives.

Are You An IMPACT DRIVEN BRAND?

If you have any of these traits, I want you to take action! Get into the work! Futurize the money, if you have to. Allow your brand to step into its future of impacting more people's lives. These are common traits of *IMPACT DRIVEN BRANDs*:

> 1. You can see what your Brand will do in the future when it thrives;

> 2. You clearly see the types of people whose lives you really care to touch and the impacts your work has on them;

> 3. You *want* to impact people lives; that is WHY your brand exists;

> 4. You might be skeptical of "Branding" because it feels "in-authentic" or "contrived" to you; regardless, you know it is

important to make your impacts and you want help "doing it right the first time;"

5. You do *not* want to become the expert, wasting money & time in trial & error growing your brand; you want an expert who listens and understands you so The Brand authentically represents you.

Is this resonating? Do you identify with this?

Might this process be a blessing to you?

Read these descriptions of entrepreneurs who are clearly ready for IMPACT DRIVEN BRANDING. Ask yourself: Are you similar?

1. *A Higher Level:* You have deep experience in your work for years; you want to take your work to a higher level -- impact more people; teach others your gift; pass it on as a legacy; step from your work into your purpose -- and you clearly see the people you'll help and how you'll touch their lives.

2. *New Service or Product:* Your work has created something new and unique to you; you can clearly see the positive impact on people's lives – a "method", curriculum, training, product, service, new way of doing something, series of signature speeches on topics of your deep expertise.

3. *Finally Doing What You Love:* You retire from a successful career. Or you decide to shift from employee to self-employed, to have your own business. You are finally "doing what you love," and you want to build your "brand" without lots of mistakes wasting time and money; you clearly see the types of individuals whose lives your work will impact. Although you are passionate and committed in your new work, you are not known as an expert. This is an *IMPACT DRIVEN BRANDING* opportunity. It requires language-of-the-brand to position your Brand so people *prefer* you.

Your Look Inside IMPACT DRIVEN BRANDING:

The 7 Steps to Ensure YOUR Brand Impacts People's Lives, and the World!

This is a summary for you, a quick guide through the *7 Steps* to read and think about, and to get started.

"Every day, we are guiding individuals' Brands using the 7 Steps, and it is beautiful thing to see each individual watch their Brand Come Alive," Rich Kozak, **RichBrands.**

STEP #1:

Imagine Your Brand *Thriving*:

You Can Clearly See the Impacts!

What can you do to put your Impact Driven Brand on Track from the Beginning?

Imagine your Brand in the future when it's *thriving*. The Brand could be you or an entity. Picture it *thriving*—successfully attracting, serving people and impacting their lives in positive ways and your successful business is *thriving*. What is it doing, actually? Is it offering 1-on-1 coaching? Group Coaching? Speaking at Events to Groups & People you want to reach? Hosting Online Virtual Events? Writing Books? Developing Clients near home? In other countries? Bringing Something New Into People's Lives? Changing Something for the Better? Contributing to Community? Write down what you see your *thriving* Brand doing in each of its three stages:

1. What is the Brand doing when it Launches?

   Pre-Launch (creating, preparing)

   Soft Launch (testing)

   Launch Day and the Launch Period (6-24 months)

2. What Does the Brand Do to Grow and Expand Its Reach (3-20+ years)

3. What Legacy Does the Brand Create and Get Credit For? (this might sound like:)
   Over time, the Brand is acknowledged by…

   The Brand is credited with…

Why is this Step Important?

It gives CLARITY of vision to your *Desired Brand*.

STEP #2:

Envision Your Highest Value Impacts:

The Who & What In Your Mind's Eye.

[At *RichBrands*, we do this step every day supporting our clients, and you can also do this important step by yourself, with your eyes closed, if you wish!]

When you think about your Brand thriving and impacting the lives of individuals and eventually groups of similar people, who are those people?

What type of person, specifically, do you clearly see in your mind's eye who you know you can impact, and you really want to impact, through your work? For each type of person you clearly see impacting, note what specifics about the individual help you identify that type of person. What are that person's demographics? Lifestyle behavior? Stage or situation in life? You might be able to clearly see more than one type of person that you know you will impact, so focus on one type of person at a time.

For each type of person that you clearly see impacting, write the *Impacts* you clearly see your work will have on that person when your brand is thriving. Consider that *Impacts* occur at increasingly higher levels. For each type of person, note the levels of *Impacts* and envision the highest-level *Impact* you can clearly see your work having on that person.

Why is this Step Important?

This Step #2 writing down specific *Impacts* provides intention and goals the Brand aspires to achieve. You get CLARITY for what your *Desired Brand* wants most to accomplish.

STEP #3:

Organize Your Desired Brand In Three Parts:

Your Desired Brand Triangle

STEP #3 provides a visual tool to guide you becoming "the Brand you must become to achieve the *Impacts* you envision" -- your *Desired Brand.*

Three parts:

> *Characteristics,*
>
> *Competencies,*
>
> *Measurable Milestones.*

Why is this Step Important?

The *Characteristics* describe the Brand so clearly that even a stranger can understand how the Brand thinks, speaks, behaves, and makes decisions. The *Characteristics* define the culture of the brand and help guide how the brand and people who represent it speak and behave, promote, write, hire, train, assess and serve clients.

The *Competencies* clearly state the results the Brand becomes known for delivering and which attract more people to the Brand.

Characteristics and *Competencies* provide guidelines and language to ensure marketing elements are aligned with the Brand and the Brand gets credit.

You achieve your Impacts sooner. Your marketing stays on track.

You get "the power of 'NEXT!' "You easily judge any idea based on how directly it supports the Characteristics you must get credit for. If it does not offer clear support, "NEXT!".

STEP #4:

Define the Characteristics Your Brand Must Become:

Breathing Life Into Your Brand

Step #4 breathes life into your *Desired Brand.* It gives your Brand authenticity reflecting what's in the heart of the Brand.

Ask yourself for each *Impact* Statement (STEP #2), "what characteristic must the Brand become in order to make this *Impact?*" Write a descriptive word or phrase that "resonates" with you. For example, if you are a health fitness brand, *must* your Brand "Validate" people's possibilities, their program or regimen you put them on, and the results produced? Then the descriptive word "Validating" might resonate with you. Or "Measuring" or "Results-Driven". You choose the word that resonates with you.

Then you answer the question, "In what ways must the Brand be *{Characteristic}*?"

Write complete sentence answers that state in clear language each of these *Aspects* of the *Characteristic*. Doing that for our "Validating" example, the *Aspects* might be:

Validating:

> *The Brand validates the person (their worth, their possibilities, their power).*

> *The Brand validates the individual's program or regimen.*

> *The Brand validates the results.*

Why is this Step So Important?

The moment your Brand has clarity of what it <u>must</u> become and get credit for in order to make its envisioned *Impacts*, it assures you that everything the Brand says and does can support the process of becoming and getting credit. Defining and *Aspecting* your *Desired Brand's Characteristics* empowers you and all who work with the Brand to ensure that every action, every piece of content, every program, every promotion, is congruent with the *Desired Brand*, without confusion or misinformation.

STEP #5:

Prioritize Categories of Expertise for Which Your Brand <u>Must</u> Get Credit:

Words for the Straight and Contrived Categories Required to Make Your Impacts.

With STEPS #1- #4 completed, you have the foundation, perspective and language you need to consider *Categories of Expertise – the categories of information for which the Brand must become known as being outstanding and for which the Brand is capable and available to speak, write an article, be interviewed as an expert, do a training, write a book or a chapter in a book, record a teaching video, etc.*

Your *Desired Brand* <u>must</u> get credit for being expert in certain *Categories* in order to make its envisioned *Impacts*. The obvious questions are:

"What are your Brand's *Categories of Expertise?*", and

"What words do we use to express your *Categories of Expertise?*", and

"Which *Category of Expertise* must you get credit for first? Second? prioritized."

Words have power. Your Brand needs that power describing its *Categories of Expertise* to come alive and attract.

Example: There is a huge difference between claiming your expertise is:

"Women's Health"

or

"Releasing Women from the Weight of Unhealthy Life"

Why? One sounds generic and the other transfers energy and has within it an *intangible Brand promise* that attracts a *Target Audience*.

Why is this Step Important?

It begins the process of creating a strategic, confidential document that gets the Brand *credit* for what makes it outstanding. It uses consistent words that transfer energy and attract *Target Audiences*. It sets your Brand apart from other competitors. And, when arranged in priority order, the *Categories of Expertise* create "stakes in the ground" that move your Brand forward, strategically.

STEP #6:

Craft Content Titles & SubTitles for Categories of Expertise:

There Are Only Two Rules; the More Your Do the More Fun It Gets.

Your Brand *must* get credit, clear and uplifting credit, for each of your *Categories of Expertise* to make its envisioned *Impacts* on people's lives. Experts provide content. So we make this easy in a way that actually turns into fun, and creates very effective *Content Titles & SubTitles*. There are only two steps, and only two rules.

First, it's easiest to focus on one *Category of Expertise* at a time and brainstorm *"topic triggers"* -- words, ideas, questions, challenges, that come to mind when you read the *Category of Expertise*. When others help you brainstorm, say "Thank you!" and go to the next step by yourself. It is totally up to you whether you use a brainstormed *topic trigger*. For example: if you say, "My first priority *Category of Expertise* is "Guiding Women To Release the Weight of Unhealthy Life" and your friend says: "Is there a method?" "Can this work for any age woman?" and "I love giraffes." You get to choose to *not* use the giraffe one because it doesn't work for you.

Second, you turn a *topic trigger* into a *Content Title & SubTitle* following two rules. Rule #1: stay congruent with the Brand's *Characteristics* (if the Brand must be "Uplifting", the Title "Why Are People So Stupid?" is incongruent.)

Rule #2: use a hook to pull them into the content without giving the answer in the *Title & SubTitle*.

"How Can a Woman Release the Weight of Unhealthy Life?

Taking this first step is the best way to start."

Why is this Step Important?

It ensures whatever content you produce *gets credit* for the *Desired Brand*.

STEP #7:

Complete Your Marketing Readiness Checklist:

Marketing At Its Best Is the Execution of Excellent Branding Strategy.

The most common reason that many Brands experience *The 6 Bad Consequences* and even *fall flat* is because most Brands have not invested in defining and languaging the Brand BEFORE they jump prematurely into lots of marketing: From Social Media postings to Facebook Lives, from LOGOs with taglines (or LOGOs *without* taglines) to Virtual Backgrounds, and from writing Speaker Bios to writing the way they tell their story or simply answer the question, "So what do you do?".

This STEP #7 prevents jumping into marketing prematurely. It will certainly help _you_ put "first things first" (one of my father's favorite phrases, and for good reason!).

Why is this Step Important?

STEP #7 is very important because it requires answering the question:

"Are all these things completed, decided, organized, *prioritized*?"

> *Target Audiences*
>
> *Brand Language*
>
> *Personality*
>
> *Voice*
>
> *Brand Competitive Positioning*
>
> *Website Presence*
>
> *Messaging Hierarchy*

What Happens when you DO This STEP?

You assure yourself that your Brand will show up and communicate with consistency, that it will get an A+ in First Impression Management (a mission critical skill area in Branding, and in marketing execution).

Imagine Your Process Completed!!

Imagine how it feels when your Desired Brand is defined with clarity!

Imagine your language aligned!

Your Brand is ready to "open its mouth" and speak in ways that come alive and attract.

Imagine your AH-HA moments during your *Power Session* and our *1-Day Intensive Workshop, "The Brand YOU Will Become".4*

Imagine completing all 7 Steps together, laughing, brainstorming, acting as sounding boards with each other in a *"Brand Accelerator Group"* that powers through the work in seven days over an 8-week period. You go from zero to 60 in 8 weeks. Imagine.

We serve clients every day at *RichBrands* and you're welcome to join us.

Do you want help? Request a ZOOM strategy Session 1-on-1 with Rich.

Email your name and cell to Rich@RichBrands.org or text 626-533-6432

Ask About:

Video Trainings Online

½-Day Personal Brand Discovery Power Session   1-on-1 with Rich

½-Day Event: Branding YOU With Impact!   Live on ZOOM

1-Day Intensive Workshop: *The Brand YOU Will Become* Live on ZOOM

7-Day Brand Accelerator Group.   Live on ZOOM

6-month Brand Launch Marketing Live on ZOOM

The IMPACT DRIVEN BRANDING Podcast

***

To contact Rich:

www.RichBrands.org

Afterword

Life and business are always a series of transitions… people, places, and things that shape who we are as individuals. Often, you never know that the next catalyst for improving your business and life is around the corner, in the next person you meet, next mentor you hire or the next book you read.

Jim Britt and Kevin Harrington have spent decades influencing individuals and entrepreneurs with strategies to grow their business, developing the right mindset and mental toughness to thrive in today's business environment and to live a better life.

Allow all you have read in this book to create a new you, to reinvent yourself and your business model if required, because every business and life level requires a different you. It is your journey to craft.

Cracking the Rich Code is a series that offers much more than a book. It is a community of like-minded influencers from around the world. A global movement. Each chapter is like opening a surprise gift, that just may contain the one idea that changes everything for you. Watch for future releases and add them to your collection. If you know of anyone who would like to be considered as a co-author for a future volume, have them email our offices at support@jimbritt.com

The individual and combined works of Jim Britt and Kevin Harrington have filled seminar rooms to maximum capacity and created a worldwide demand. If you get the opportunity to attend one of their live events, jump at the chance. You'll be glad you did.

If you are a coach, speaker, consultant of entrepreneur and would like to get the details about becoming a coauthor in the next Cracking the Rich Code book in the series, contact Jim Britt at support@jimbritt.com or watch this video and schedule a time to speak with Jim: https://www.richcode.club/beacoauthor/

STRUGGLING WITH MONEY ISSUES?

Check out Jim's latest program "Cracking the Rich Code" which focuses on the subconscious programs influencing one's financial success, that keeps most living a life of mediocrity. This powerful four-month program is designed to change one's relationship with money and reset your money programming to that of the wealthy. More details at: www.CrackingTheRichCode.com

To Schedule Jim Britt or Kevin Harrington as a featured speaker at your next convention or special event, online or live, email: support@jimbritt.com

Master each moment as they become hours that become days.

Make it a great life!

Your legacy awaits.

STAY IN TOUCH

www.JimBritt.com

www.JimBrittCoaching.com

www.CrackingTheRichCode.com

www.KevinHarrington.tv

https://www.richcode.club/beacoauthor/

For daily strategies and insights from top coaches,

speakers and entrepreneurs, join us at:

THE RICH CODE CLUB---FREE members site.

www.TheRichCodeClub.com

CPSIA information can be obtained
at www.ICGtesting.com
Printed in the USA
BVHW040023100122
625855BV00014B/448